Accounting Sustainable Development: International Advancements at Macro and Micro Level

Edited by

Edoardo Pizzoli
Department of Finance
University of Luxembourg
Luxembourg, Luxembourg

Accounting Sustainable Development:
International Advancements at Macro and Micro Level

Editor: Edoardo Pizzoli

ISBN (Online): 979-8-89881-357-4

ISBN (Print): 979-8-89881-358-1

ISBN (Paperback): 979-8-89881-359-8

Published by Bentham Science Publishers Pte. Ltd. Singapore,

in collaboration with Eureka Conferences, USA.

First published in 2026.

Bentham Science Publishers Pte. Ltd.
No. 9 Raffles Place
Office No. 26-01
Singapore 048619
Singapore
Email: subscriptions@benthamscience.net

BENTHAM SCIENCE

CONTENTS

FOREWORD

Sustainable development is a global priority. Various policy measures have long been proposed to ensure this model of development. United Nations member states also adopted the Sustainable Development Agenda in 2015 to achieve the Sustainable Development Goals (SDGs) by 2031. A number of indicators to track the progress have also been identified and countries, regularly and systematically, seek to monitor them. Unfortunately, though halfway through, still most of the countries have not been able to measure all the indicators set out to verify achievements.

The indicators identified are isolated and do not necessarily follow the rigorous approach adopted by the UN System of National Accounts (SNA). There is a need to develop a *sustainable accounting framework* that can be universally adopted and may provide reliable estimates for effective policy-making and implementation. In addition, sectoral and regional dimensions also need to be addressed through satellite accounts.

ICAAS 2021 organized by the Luxembourg Statistical Society has done a great job by bringing the experts together to apply their minds and share their experiences on this topic. The present volume comprehensively documents the views, experience, and suggestions on how to follow the path for developing sustainability accounting systems.

I am sure that this volume will be of immense value for researchers and official statisticians in the field in their day-to-day work.

I would highly recommend all the students, practitioners, and academics to consult this volume which comprehensively addresses both theoretical and practical issues of sustainable accounting.

Ashish Kumar
United Nations Statistical
Institute for Asia and the Pacific, Japan
and Central Statistics Office
Ministry of Statistics & Programme Implementation
Government of India

PREFACE

This volume is one of the outcomes of an international conference on accounting and assessment in statistics (ICAAS), that took place in 2021 in Luxembourg and was led by the Luxembourg Statistics Society (SLS) in collaboration with several research, accounting and statistical institutions.

The main topic introduced and discussed in the volume concern current developments in this area of measurement, between research and real-world professional applications, in response to the demand for more quantitative information in order to meet the challenges of sustainability.

Several contributions and points of view of specialists in the field are reported in three sections: the present and future of the accounting system for sustainable development, specific focuses on growing accounting sub-systems and finally, some example of economic sustainability issues for policy makers.

We hope that this volume will contribute to the enhancement of research and applications of accounting systems that can support countries to rapidly reach a sustainable development path. In this attempt, the theoretical and practical applications presented by the contributors to this volume open up interesting prospects for further development of the accounting tools used to process and present numerical data.

Edoardo Pizzoli
Department of Finance
University of Luxembourg
Luxembourg, Luxembourg

Special Thanks

"Special thanks to Jang Schiltz (University of Luxembourg), Christophe Ley (SLS) and Dario Buono (Eurostat)".

APPRECIATION BY THE SOCIÉTÉ LUXEMBOURGEOISE DE STATISTIQUE (SLS)

The Luxembourg Statistical Society is very glad to see this new publication on "Sustainability accounting" with contributions from statisticians and researchers from our scientific community. The publication was possible thanks to the results of the first international conference we promoted in 2021 on accounting and assessment in statistics (ICAAS).

As a Society we are closely following the important ongoing process of revision in official statistics, concerning national and regional accounts (SNA at UN level and ESA at EU level), to meet the need to produce indicators on pressing policy objective for the next decades.

Quite in parallel, a similar process of innovation is underway in the corporate and financial sector accounts to disclose information on sustainability, mainly under the pressure of EU legislation in Europe. These accounts continue to be the basic source of data providing information to statistical offices. Statistical accounts need and benefit from this continuous flow of data; that is why there is almost the same process at micro-accounting level connected to the macro-statistical one.

This is definitely an important era of innovation in accounting and statistics that will change the future information system and official statistics to support the UN SDGs and sustainability challenges globally. In two large political areas, the European Union and the Federal Republic of India, as can be seen from the contributions published in this book, the process of change is already rapidly underway. The analyses and summary results reported on some specific applications in the satellite accounts provide a vision for the future.

The LSS would like to thank the institutions and people involved for their input. We hope that this publication will provide a useful contribution to academic research and its pipeline in this important area of statistics.

Christophe Ley
Société Luxembourgeoise de Statistique (SLS)
Luxembourg, Luxembourg

ACKNOWLEDGEMENTS

1. Institutions:

Eurostat, EU

The Federation of European National Statistical Societies (FENStatS)

Indian Association for Research in National Income and Wealth (IARNIW)

Institut national de la Statistique et des études économiques (STATEC) - Luxembourg

Istituto Nazionale di Statistica (ISTAT) - Italy

PricewaterhouseCoopers International Limited (PWC) Luxembourg

Société Luxembourgeoise de Statistique (SLS)

2. Technical support:

Easypress Technologies, UK

Kernel Tech Srl, Romenia

University of Luxembourg

3. Contributors:

The following authors contributed to this publication. Excerpts from their interventions to the ICAAS Conference (https://icaas.eu) are included in the chapters below:

Battellini, Federica (Istat, Italy) – Chapter 6

Bhanumati, P (National Statistics Office India) – Chapter 4

De la Fuente, Artro (Eurostat, EU) – Chapter 1

Dogniez, Nathalie (PWC-Luxembourg) – Chapter 2

Lori, Massimo (Istat, Italy) – Chapter 5

Orsini, Chiara (Istat, Italy) – Chapter 5

Piersante, Angela (Eurostat, EU) – Chapter 7

Pizzoli, Edoardo (University of Luxembourg) – Chapter 1, 2, 3, 8, 9, 10, 11

Pop, Cecilia (Eurostat, EU) – Chapter 7

Radermacher, Walter (FENStatS, Luxembourg) – Chapter 1

Sharma, Rajiv (IARNIW, India) – Chapter 1

Tudini, Angelica (Istat, Italy) – Chapter 6

Valdimarsdóttir, Viktoría (University of Luxembourg) – Chapter 2

Verrinder, John (Eurostat, EU) – Chapter 1

INTRODUCTION

The application of the objective of "sustainability" to development is a sort of theoretical concept that requires policymakers to dispose of a complex set of information as multiple dimensions are involved. As set out in the UN Sustainable Development Goals (SDGs), along with traditional economic targets of development, environmental and social matters have become equally relevant for "sustainability" and as well as being closely interrelated.

The accounting framework that we propose in this publication, provided its systemic approach, appears to be highly suited to address this general policy objective.

There has been quite a long evolution in the history of bookkeeping, from the first accountants in Mesopotamian times in the XX century B.C., who started putting numbers in columns to calculate an addition and the set-up of the first input-output table, to the Italian merchants in the late Middle Ages, when the more complex double-entry was invented in accounting, up to modern times, after the Great Depression of the '30s, with the introduction of National Accounts, and the Second World War, with the developments in computer science and the new information technologies (Edwards *et al.*, 2021).

Today, difficulties that we thought to be a "physical" limit to the possibilities of accounting seem to have been overcome by information technology: the amount of data storage, the speed of data processing, the modalities of presentation of accounts and the interaction with human beings. Computers are playing a crucial role in accounting as arithmetic and zero errors in calculations are in the core of computational systems. That is why the system of accounts is expanding beyond belief and at an astonishing speed.

Proof of this are, for example, the subsystems of satellite accounts in national accounts, which were already conceived in the '60s and widely applicable today.

This publication presents the ongoing accounting "revolution" and discusses some key applications, at a micro-company and macro-regional level, with experts in the field, providing some insights on future developments that are expected in the coming years. In addition to the growing IT technology, an acceleration of research and applications by accountants in different areas is expected.

A community of field researchers, statisticians, accountants, professionals and IT experts involved will be at the heart of, leading, the development of this new modern era for the accounting systems.

List of Contributors

Arturo De La Fuente	Eurostat, Luxembourg, Luxembourg
Angelica Tudini	Department for Statistical Production, ISTAT, Rome, Italy
Angela Piersante	Eurostat, Luxembourg, Luxembourg
Chiara Orsini	Department for Statistical Production, ISTAT, Rome, Italy
Cecilia Pop	Eurostat, Luxembourg, Luxembourg
Edoardo Pizzoli	Department of Finance, University of Luxembourg, Luxembourg, Luxembourg
Federica Battellini	Department for Statistical Production, ISTAT, Rome, Italy
John Verrinder	Eurostat, Luxembourg, Luxembourg
Nathalie Dogniez	AWM Research Centre, PWC-Luxembourg, Luxembourg, Luxembourg
Massimo Lori	Department for Statistical Production, ISTAT, Rome, Italy
P. Bhanumati	National Statistical Office, New Delhi, India
Rajiv Sharma	IARNIW, New Delhi, India
Viktoría Valdimarsdóttir	Department of Social Sciences, University of Luxembourg, Luxembourg, Luxembourg
Walter Radermacher	FENStatS, Luxembourg, Luxembourg

PART I: Present and Future of the Accounting Systems for Sustainable Development

CHAPTER 1

The Revision Process of National Accounts at the EU and UN Level

Edoardo Pizzoli[1,*], **Walter Radermacher**[2], **John Verrinder**[3], **Arturo De La Fuente**[3] and **Rajiv Sharma**[4]

[1] *Department of Finance, University of Luxembourg, Luxembourg, Luxembourg*

[2] *FENStatS, Luxembourg, Luxembourg*

[3] *Eurostat, Luxembourg, Luxembourg*

[4] *IARNIW, New Delhi, India*

Abstract: At its 51st session, in 2020, the United Nations Statistical Commission (UNSC) started the process of revision of the 2008 System of National Accounts (SNA) for adoption by the Commission in 2025 ("Towards 2025 SNA"; see website UNSTAT 2).

This is a periodic review of the system at an international level, to update the accounts and introduce into the system new challenging topics, such as 'Sustainable development', which require systematisation of the relevant data to achieve the level of coherence needed for policy purposes. The views of the UN, the EU and other countries, such as India, are reported in this chapter.

After recalling the key role of SNA in official statistics, the revision process at the UN level is resumed, with a focus on the main extension, led by Eurostat, on the environmental dimension of sustainability.

The chapter concludes with some remarks on the prospects of this extension for the Indian subcontinent and the Arab countries of the Persian Gulf.

Keywords: Beyond GDP, Data, Digitalization, Environmental-economic accounting, National accounts, Official statistics, Revision process, Sustainable development.

* **Corresponding author Edoardo Pizzoli:** Department of Finance, University of Luxembourg, Luxembourg, Luxembourg; E-mail: edoardo.pizzoli@uni.lu

INTRODUCTION

The present chapter examines the progress and direction taken in updating the SNA with respect to the reflection of broader environmental, sustainability and welfare considerations.

Links to other statistical systems are indicated, showing how relevant supplementary tables can be presented in a 'whole system' approach.

An important insight for Eurostat concerns the System of Environmental Economic Accounting (SEEA). A summary and the results achieved in the EU and some other non-EU countries are introduced at the end of this chapter.

THE SYSTEM OF NATIONAL ACCOUNTS IN OFFICIAL STATISTICS

The system of National Accounts plays an important role in official statistics and is constantly evolving with technological progress and the growing demand for indicators for policy needs. National statistical offices are the public institutions that manage this system and governments devote specific attention to them. In the following paragraphs, we will see the specific function of the accounts and the expected developments of the official statistics.

Accounts in the Factory of Statistics and the Role of Government

In statistics in general, there is a process of reducing the complexity of information. Several stages can be identified, with an active role of public authorities, national and international, to define, standardize and regulate statistics. One could distinguish two main 'blocks' in the statistical process which go from the quantification of phenomena to the final policy decisions (Fig. **1**).

In the first phase, we move from raw data, through basic statistics, accounts and then highly aggregated indicators. In the second phase comes the interpretation of these facts: we extract information in order to feed and to 'augment' the policy of the decision-making process. In the first phase, we reduce the context, we codify the data and, in the second phase, we decode and add context to interpret what we have learned *via* statistics.

Accounting systems are the middle layer, creating a kind of halfway from micro, very detailed statistics with a 'granularity', to a consistent framework which then also enables us to create a smaller set of macro indicators. This is in line with the reduction tunnel we have drawn from complexity to reduced and condensed information. We could say that basic statistics are just a collection of 'stones', even if we sort them according to their 'colours': these would then be economic statistics, social statistics and so forth. With them, we are not really able to see the overall picture. This only comes if we put them together in a kind of framework: we bring a structured order into the collection of stones, which are the basic statistics. We find a similar role for accounts at different levels: from companies to regions, to national and supranational political unions.

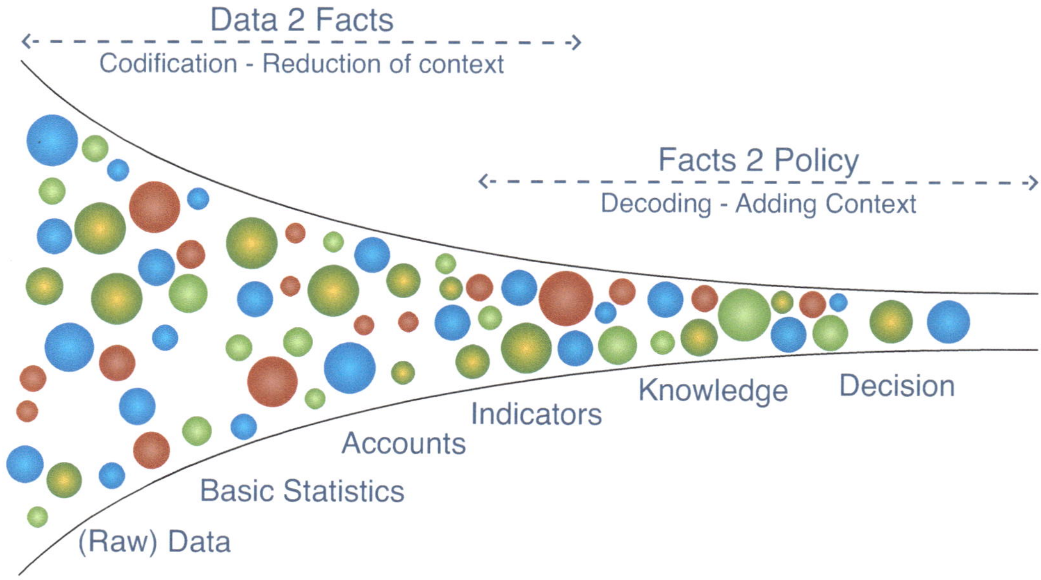

Fig. (1). Reducing complexity: stages from data to policy.

In the opposite direction, we could distinguish from policy to data. This is very popular in many countries and now in the European Commission with the data strategy, with the objective of EU digitalization. These policies that address data issues very rarely include an explicit policy for statistics: a statistical framework and statistical governance, which is not the same as a policy for raw data, markets and the economy of data.

Accounting in Official Statistics

Official statistics has the particular aim to create a common language for the public. The backbone of official statistics is, therefore, standardization, *i.e.*, having a statistical production with standards of quality, comparability and ultimately a low level of required statistical literacy (which results in equality and democracy). The aggregated accounts are an essential framework in this process of standardization and production of information for society (Radermacher, 2020).

Note that this is exactly the opposite of what we do in 'data science', where the goal is to have individualized statistical production. In official statistics, we have a 'factory 'of statistics with several processes: design, production, communication and dissemination, use of statistics for decision-making and feedback to design. Official statistics are an 'infrastructure', such as, for example, public railways, which need to be maintained and other actions are required with respect to policies than just opening the market for data scientists.

Expected Developments

We have to bear in mind when we talk about the statistical programs for the coming years, that we already have the SDGs (17 goals, 169 targets and 231 indicators) outlining the main themes for the future, even if there are too many indicators to help policymakers.

Human societies have to face globalization and global risk (WEF, 2022). The planet is at risk of heading towards a greenhouse state, but the economy also is at risk, for example, in Ireland, in the EU, some years ago, multinationals moved from one country to another, creating radical changes at the local level communities. There are issues not only for the economy itself but also for measurement. This is a difficult situation for official statistics (NSF, 2019).

In the history of official statistics, we moved through several periods: we are now moving after a previous phase, with the computer age, to a new phase (O.S. 4.0) with machine-produced data and statistics (Radermacher, 2020). Data alone cannot drive the official statistics production which instead must be oriented toward the information needed. To do this, we need new partners in co-planning and co-designing statistics, evolving production to meet the mentioned policy objectives of sustainability.

The new accounts for the future, considering the critical role they have in framing the data, must follow these new inputs from science and civil society.

UPDATING NATIONAL ACCOUNTS STANDARDS - A 'WHOLE SYSTEM' APPROACH

Worldwide statistical standards for national accounts are established in the System of National Accounts (SNA; UNSTAT, 2009, 2025). The SNA has progressively developed since its first edition in 1953 to adapt to changes in the economy and the needs of users of accounts, but has remained largely focused on its perceived core task as a coherent, consistent and integrated set of macroeconomic accounts to measure economic activity. The most widely recognised summary measure within the national accounts - Gross Domestic Product (GDP) - is an aggregate of economic activity that is closely followed for economic policy purposes.

National accountants recognise that there has been increasing interest amongst users over many years to view measures of economic activity within the broader context of society and the environment. There has been criticism that 'narrow' measures such as GDP do not reflect developments in sustainability and welfare and an overreliance of policymakers on GDP inevitably diminishes their attention to these aspects. National accountants recognise the need to react to "Beyond GDP" criticism (for example, the recommendations of the 2009 'Stiglitz-Sen-Fitoussi Commission'), both to remain relevant and to reflect the growing richness of available data (Stiglitz *et al*., 2009; OECD, 2018).

One could consider three broad options for addressing this issue:

Option 1 - Include existing national accounts data within a broader 'Dashboard' of indicators released by statistical authorities, so that users can see the evolution of traditional indicators alongside other indicators of sustainability and well-being from outside the national accounts system.

Option 2 - Encourage the development of supplementary systems of accounts (for example, for the environment), which are clearly linked to the national accounts but provide greater detail and possibly extend some of the concepts in national accounts to reflect sustainability and well-being.

Option 3 - Revise the so-called 'core system' of national accounts, so that traditional indicators such as GDP are more reflective of the evolution of sustainability and well-being.

There is no 'one size fits all' solution to this question. Option 1 is implementable in a shorter term and is already widely used, although good communication with users is essential, particularly those who look for 'one number'. Options 2 and 3 might even overlap to the extent that the SNA framework is considered to encompass more than just traditional economic accounts.

The 2008 SNA underwent a lengthy update process and a new version of the SNA was adopted in 2025. (see website UNSTAT 1). The update process has clearly recognised the importance of addressing well-being and sustainability issues with a dedicated 'Task Team'. 'Guidance Notes' prepared during the process are progressively issued for global consultation and several notes will be highly relevant, notably (a full list of Guidance Notes have been can be found on the website UNSTAT 2):

A. In relation to the framework:
- A broader SNA framework for well-being and sustainability.
- Terminology and branding of the economic accounting statistical standards.

B. In relation to specific topics on well-being and sustainability:
- Distribution of household income, consumption saving and wealth.
- Unpaid household service work.
- Labour, education and human capital.
- Health and social conditions.
- Economic ownership and depletion of natural resources.
- Emissions permits: the atmosphere as an asset.
- Accounting for biological resources.
- Renewable energy resources.

The SNA is an 'integrated system' and users strongly appreciate the consistency that this brings to the data with the use of common terminologies, definitions and classifications. Reference is made in the SNA (Chapter 20) to 'satellite accounts' and other extensions and there are also separate accounts described in their handbooks, which are either aligned with SNA (for example, the Balance of Payments and the Government Finance Statistics Manual) or are conceptual extensions of it (*e.g.* the System of Environmental-Economic Accounting; UNSTAT, 2014). The latter systems are widespread across countries, whereas the development of satellite accounts has often been patchy, followed by countries where there is a particular sectoral interest (*e.g.*, tourism) and frequently suffering from a lack of devoted data sources.

During the SNA upgrade process, it was recognised that the SNA needed to develop from a 'core and satellites' approach towards a more integrated set of economic, social and environmental accounts. In some cases, recommendations are being considered which would introduce greater attention to welfare (*e.g.*, distribution of income, consumption and wealth) and the environment (depletion, ecosystems) in the 'economic accounts'. In other cases, supplementary systems in the social domain (notably for unpaid household work, human capital and health and social conditions) are being set out to bring greater prominence to their links to economic accounts.

The eventual challenge will be to bring together the wealth of additional information generated and link it together clearly for users. Here, the communication aspects of the SNA update process will be important, with respect to terminology and presentation and should be considered at least as relevant to the success of the future SNA as the conceptual developments under discussion.

AN EXTENSION OF ESA: THE SYSTEM OF ENVIRONMENTAL-ECONOMIC ACCOUNTING (SEEA)

The following are the key features of environmental accounting in the UN system of accounts, with specific application to the environmental accounts in the EU statistics system. Future developments are introduced, considering the latest works on experimental ecosystem accounts.

Environmental Accounts

The System of Environmental-Economic Accounting (SEEA) is a conceptual framework and a system of tables and satellites, similar to the system of National Accounts (SNA). This system integrates economic and environmental data in a coherent way, allowing consistency between the SNA and the environmental accounts.

The power of this integrated system is to provide data on the environmental impact of economic activity, facilitating economic-environmental analyses.

The strong interrelation between the economy and the environment can be clearly represented in the following picture (Fig. **2**):

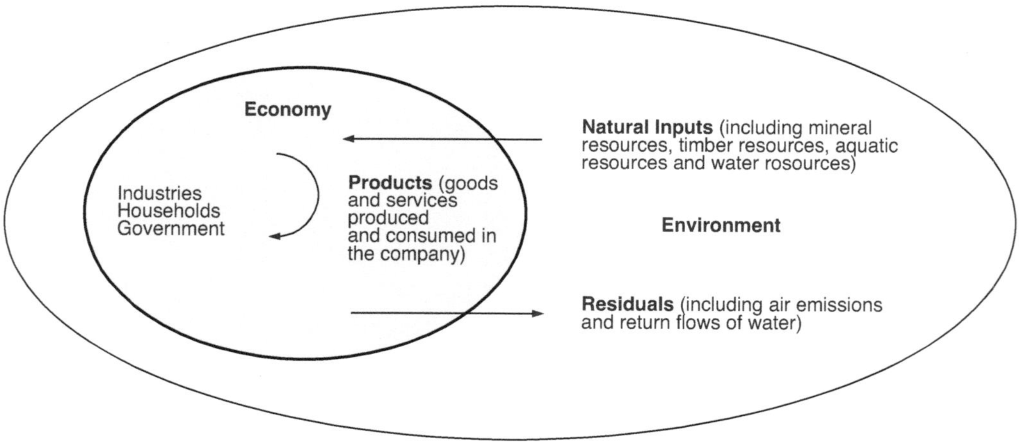

Fig. (2). Economic and environmental systems.

In our society and as individuals, we rely on a regular flow of new products created to satisfy our consumer lifestyle. These products are made from natural resources extracted from the environment. After use, residuals are frequently disposed of or discharged into the environment.

These actions go under the "radar" of official statistics of national accounts and production statistics.

At a time, there are two types of accounts, the Central Framework (CF) and the Environmental-Economic Accounts (EEA), both integrated with the SNA, albeit with a different level of maturity. The SEEA CF, which is within the SNA production and assets boundary, includes physical environmental accounts, measuring flows between the economy and the environment (water, materials, waste, *etc.*). Furthermore, it describes the environmental activity, measuring the environmentally-related flows inside the economy (green jobs, environmental taxes, investments, *etc.*).

A third system of accounts, the SEEA ecosystem accounts, goes beyond SNA boundaries and is still experimental. Ecosystems produce streams of services and natural assets with value. Specific accounts in this system allow to the production of EU geographical maps and tables.

Environmental accounts construct several information systems about the environment: GHG emissions, energy emissions, taxes and fossil fuels, and jobs in renewable energy. The system is integrated and this is a necessary feature to understand trade-offs. This integration is also useful to enhance the quality of estimations. In complex systems, such as economies or ecosystems, because there are so many interrelations at different levels, multiple integrated accounts are needed to get the full picture. Studying just one ecosystem at one single level provides answers, but they may be misleading if isolated from the rest of the system.

From a statistical perspective, we have to consider that accounting is a product, included in a chain of statistical production. Data sources are adjusted and aligned to definitions and classifications across environmental domains. The results from accounts are not identical to the data sources on which they are based and this output can be used in different ways. This sequence in data and statistics can be represented with the following pyramid (Fig. **3**):

We can think about several possible uses of environmental accounts. They are naturally suited for environmental extensions of national accounts, 'going beyond GDP'; analysis of the efficiency in the use of natural resources (resource efficiency and energy efficiency, water intensity, circular economy, *etc.*); measures of "environmental growth" (jobs, taxes, *etc.*); to produce a dashboard of indicators (to monitor SDGs) and modelling: climate change (*e.g.* carbon footprints), use of natural resources (*e.g.* material footprints), interdependencies and relations (*e.g.* consumption and jobs, taxation and pollution, *etc.*).

SEEA in the EU: What Has Been Achieved

In the EU, we have nearly three decades of experience with environmental accounts and they are no longer experimental statistics.

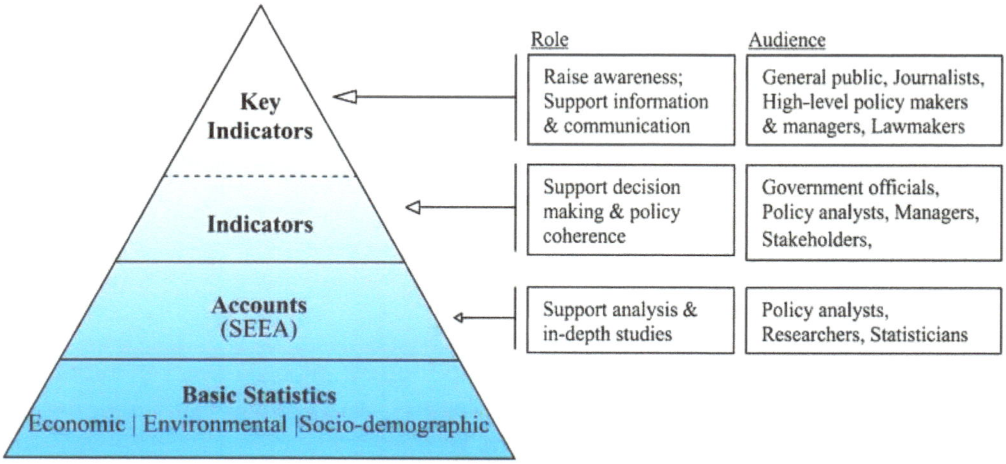

Fig. (3). Accounts in the official statistical production system.

At the moment, there are two pillars at the base of the implementation of SEEA in the EU and the development of the European environmental accounts: the European Strategy on Environmental Accounts (ESEA) 2019-2023 (Eurostat, 2019a; Eurostat, 2021) and the Regulation No 691/2011 on European Environmental Accounts (EEA) (EU, 2021b).

The European strategy is a high-level agreement with producers in EU Member States that establishes priorities for 2019-2023 and identifies areas of work beyond 2023.

Regulation No 691/2011 is an EU law on how to compile and transmit the data to Eurostat, setting the quality standards. This statistical production is applicable in Member States and other European countries. At the moment there are 6 environmental accounts considered in the regulation, with 5 possibly more currently under discussion.

Based on that, in Eurostat, there are databases for more than 30 European countries on several environmental topics and annual data collection, on mandatory (for the 6 accounts by EU law) and voluntary accounts (for 2 more). The Handbooks and the compilation tools are available for all. Eurostat is gearing up towards the development of global SEEA databases together with other international agencies, including UNSD and OECD.

The System of European Environmental Accounts

At the moment, in the European statistical system, there are two groups of environmental accounts: physical and monetary accounts (Fig. **4**).

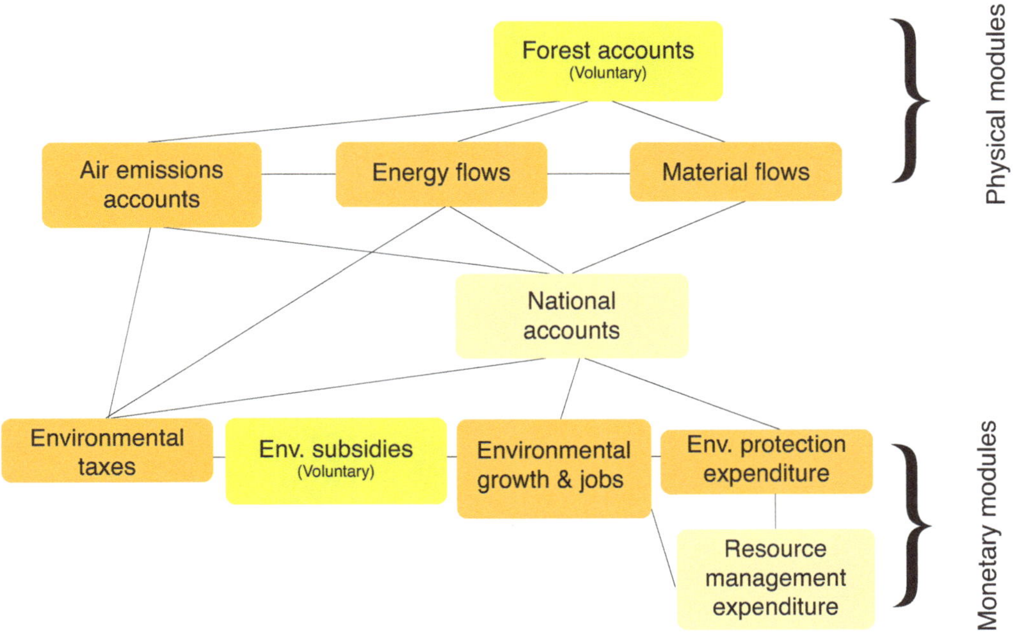

Fig. (4). European environmental accounts.

The accounts in orange are mandatory (3 since 2014 and 3 since 2017), the accounts in yellow are voluntary, while "resource management expenditure" is in development, that is, the methodology is available, but there is still no data collection.

Physical accounts are about flows between the environment and the economy (extraction of natural resources, residuals and waste). Monetary accounts are about production, expenditure, taxes and other items of the environmental sector in the economy.

Both of them, physical and monetary accounts, are based on SEEA CF.

In addition to them, there are new proposals under discussion among EU member countries: forest accounts (which are currently voluntary but will become mandatory), environmental subsidies and water accounts (currently voluntary), account for natural resources management (with 'green investment' on renewable energy, materials recovery and energy efficiency) and finally, ecosystem accounts.

Ecosystem Accounts

Ecosystem accounts are the latest development in the environmental system of accounts, which allow us to go beyond the definition of capital in SNA. With them, we extend the SNA production boundary to include natural capital and services of ecosystems (*e.g.*, carbon sequestration).

This new system includes assets such as biological (both cultivated and natural) and water resources, which produce services for us: for example, carbon sequestration by forests, flood protection, crop pollination, *etc.*

These extended assets provide ecosystem services and benefits used in economic and other human activities, which is a rather euphemistic formulation for services on which human and other lives depend.

In the accounts, we can differentiate provisioning services (such as nutrition, materials and energy), regulation services (such as carbon sequestration, water conditions and disease control) and cultural services (such as enjoying the landscape, trekking and spiritual). An example is forests that provide timber, a carbon sink and the pleasure of visiting a natural park.

These ecosystem services, as in the previous modules of environmental accounts, can also be measured in physical and monetary terms. A system of accounts will be available in the coming years.

THE DEVELOPMENT OF THE SNA TOWARDS SATELLITE ACCOUNTS IN THE NON-EUROPEAN CONTEXT: INDIA AND ARAB COUNTRIES OF THE PERSIAN GULF

This is a final reflection from India's perspective, in light of the developments in the accounting system observed in the UN and EU. This observation point allows us to understand what future developments could be in the rest of the world in the near future.

A Non-EU Perspective of SNA

The development that is being experienced in the system of national accounts in Europe, with growing satellite accounts to be able to support sustainability policies, has a different weight with different challenges to meet from the perspective of non-European countries.

If we observe from India what is taking place in the rest of the world, there is a strong feeling that there will be significant changes by 2025. This may not be called now a "system of national accounts" and it may be something like "integrated economic accounts" with a lot of Global Infrastructures (GIs) and digital inputs to be in that. The name itself may just expand the horizon of this whole system.

India and the Rest of the World *Versus* the EU

Coming back to the European experience of the satellite accounts, there is now a growing realization all over the non-European and US countries. Especially at the state and city level, within the EU, there is a very tight regulation regime and, plus, somewhat "luxury" to be implemented in smaller countries, so most of the developments are done in the central offices.

In the Indian subcontinent, the federation of states covers a geographically large region with a National Statistical Office (NSO) that depends on various Ministries and departments, with similar setups at union and state government levels. To bring all data to the National Statistics Office is a really challenging task. From the policy perspective, we have the subject specialist ministries, like the Ministry of Tourism that deals with the "tourism satellite account" or if we consider the "health account", the Ministry of Health takes care of it. Naturally, the NSO is in close coordination and works with them, but most of the time, the feeling is that the subject specialists are in those ministries. Furthermore, they have engaged many professional institutes and bodies specialized in those subjects. They have, for example, health accounts, and local professionals in this area that have a big national health resource: the "National Health Systems Resource Center".

There is a growing realization from statisticians that, unlike the central framework, which provides a lot of flexibility to bring the satellite accounts into the fold, the "real" phenomena are happening very fast.

The better part of the policymakers is more comfortable with the non-monetary data for social welfare and this well-being, which is showing now wellness and other measurements, such as human capital, that is essential.

Satellite accounts fortunately, provide both the parts for national accounting by adhering to the national accounting approach and the framework on that, to bring the numbers consistently. But the real challenge is the monetization of this site, which requires a lot of resources.

That is what is happening in this part of the world's statistics, showing a different situation than in European countries.

The Innovation Process and Digitalization in the Accounting Systems

Accountancy capacity building and innovation are demanding at the macro level but also at the level of the various players in the economy.

We understand, for example, from the national accounts point of view, the issue of keeping the coherence of information. What makes the system of national, regional and satellite accounts stronger is that there is a common set of definitions, classifications and standard forms for the accounts. This infrastructure and its improvements provide standardization and stability to the system, afterward making it easier to read and use data.

A further improvement may come during the pandemic period when there was much pressure on digitalization because, whether it was education, health consultation, or commercial activities, everything may have to be introduced through IT systems.

So, the processes are changing very fast with a lot of competition in the markets.

India, fortunately, has a good IT stronghold, so maybe the accounting system can improve significantly. They are very closely following what is happening in the world and, as a surprise for Europe, some contributions that may impact the accounting system may come.

CONCLUSION

The process of periodic updating SNA and ESA is progressing rapidly at the level of the United Nations and in the European Union; new accounts will be made public during this decade.

It is clear that National Accounts, as an integrated system covering different domains, which grew around the historical developments on macroeconomic description carried out after the great depression of the 1930s, have a very high potential for extension to also cover the issues of 'sustainable development'.

Specifically, accounts on the environmental dimension have been developed starting from Europe and industrialized countries, but, as we have seen, in the case of India, other countries that are highly sensitive to the environment and affected by climate change dedicate great attention to them.

The accounting approach and methodology developed so far will continue to be widely expanded and applied in official statistics in the coming decades.

An extraordinary development of this system, linked to new IT technologies, is expected soon, especially in the newly developing countries alongside Europe and North America.

CHAPTER 2

Measuring Sustainable Development for Business: The EU'S Experience in Taxonomy and Non-Financial Reporting

Edoardo Pizzoli[1,*], **Nathalie Dogniez**[2] and **Viktoría Valdimarsdóttir**[3]

[1] *Department of Finance, University of Luxembourg, Luxembourg, Luxembourg*

[2] *AWM Research Centre, PWC-Luxembourg, Luxembourg*

[3] *Department of Social Sciences, University of Luxembourg, Luxembourg, Luxembourg*

Abstract: Accounting at corporate level has a long and consolidated history and is nowadays highly standardised internationally. Financial and fiscal accounts are the core part of corporate information systems, but the emerging policy needs in recent decades and market pressure from stakeholders and consumers of their products are putting pressure on 'traditional' corporate accounting.

This chapter introduces the two main developments underway at the EU community level, stimulated and, at the same time, supported by specific EU regulations. A new so-called 'taxonomy' is being developed and implemented in Europe. The relationship with the sustainability objectives set at the political level for the business sector will be explained. A second important innovation concerns 'sustainable' reporting, *i.e.* a new form of non-financial accounting and presentation of the social and environmental impacts of business companies' activity.

This chapter is an introduction to this area of accounting which will see important and rapid development in the near future.

Keywords: Business accounting, Corporate information system, Non-financial reporting, Sustainability reporting, Sustainable development goals, Taxonomy.

INTRODUCTION

The accounting entry that is part of the information system of units, financial and non-financial companies, operating in the business sector is evolving very rapidly worldwide, under the pressure of regional policies (mainly in the European Union,

* **Corresponding author Edoardo Pizzoli:** Department of Finance, University of Luxembourg, Luxembourg, Luxembourg; E-mail: edoardo.pizzoli@uni.lu

in North America, and some Asia Pacific countries) and the overall trade environment. Stakeholders and investors are reshaping their choices following new business opportunities and a new demand for information is coming from the progressive society, culture, and concerns.

Nowadays, several challenges well summarized by the UN Sustainable Development Goals (SDGs) are at the core of the collective interest, at global and local levels, and there is a growing awareness on the part of individuals.

The accounting system at the company level, which underpins the process of disclosing corporate information to the public, is being reshaped with the new legal requirements, especially in the EU.

In this chapter, two main stimuli for a new accounting system by EU legislation are discussed: the 'Taxonomy Regulation' of 2020 (EU Regulation 2020/852) and the amended 'Accounting Directive' of 2013 (Directive 2013/34/EU) onwards (EU, 2020; EU, 2021a). This is a specific sub-system, similar to the standard financial accounts system, with the recording and framing of new corporate data, to produce consistent information and to allow the calculation of indicators required for business reporting on sustainable development.

INNOVATIONS IN BUSINESS AND FINANCIAL ACCOUNTING: EU TAXONOMY AND NEW DATA SOURCES FOR THE NATIONAL SYSTEMS

EU Taxonomy Regulation and Definition

While usually, regulations on the business and financial sector can be problematic policy instruments, the EU Taxonomy regulation, and delegated acts are really moving in the right direction and there is the hope that there will be no 'road-blockers' in this way.

The EU environmental taxonomy is a framework to discern when an economic activity can be considered environmentally sustainable. That is the general definition and also the purpose of regulation. Unfortunately, we realise that market operators find difficulties in implementing this regulation. That is why specific training on that topic is necessary for the different companies in the financial sector, starting by explaining what the EU taxonomy is.

Economic Activities not "Taxonomy Eligible"

As we can see, the taxonomy definition is not of what would allow an "easy" identification of a sustainable asset because there is no definition of

Environmental, Social, and Governance (ESG) assets. What would be a "good" ESG investment is somehow relative, because there are different sets of values and priorities at the company level.

It is not even a tool to classify a company because 'sustainability' is a concept really down to the economic activity. If a company has several activities (primary, secondary, and ancillary), we would need to drill down and break down. We would say that the turnover or the Capital Expenditures (CapEx) of the companies, into its different sectors of activity or sub-sectors, account within this classification.

Finally, taxonomy is not either a sector classification: we may have only certain activities that are named as being 'taxonomy eligible'. This is just because certain criteria have been defined and satisfied for these activities.

Of course, there are very green activities for climate change. In practice, we have more 'enabling' activities, that allow other activities to make a substantial contribution to the taxonomy objectives, whereas some very broad activities would not be covered. In the meanwhile, an activity can be indicated as eligible which means that we have a framework to analyse whether the way a company is performing that activity is environmentally sustainable or not. It is just a starting point.

Climate Change Objectives and Measurement Criteria

The objectives that have been covered so far, bearing in mind that we have only the first step of the taxonomy being delivered, are about "climate change". There are about little more than 90 activities which are focusing on the actions that are major contributors to the reduction of greenhouse gas emissions or the enabling sector.

How does EU Taxonomy work? The regulation defines six environmental objectives and, for the time being, the EU has the framework for the first two: "climate change mitigation" and "climate change adaptation". For each activity that has been defined, we have rules that are as much as possible objectives, scientific-based and quantitative, to evaluate whether an entity's activity, the way the activity is being undertaken by the company can be considered as contributing substantially to the environmental objectives. We have what is called the Technical Screening Criteria (TSC), that define a matrix. Very often this will be in terms of greenhouse gas emissions and the threshold. Usually, it will be like a relative measure to the sector, but it is different from one sector to the other, plus a certain number of additional criteria, to ensure that when an activity, for instance, is targeting climate change mitigation, it does not harm the other five environmental dimensions (like water waste, biodiversity or climate change adaptation).

When an activity has passed the test, we also have to ensure that the company is following certain minimum "social safeguards", and then we can consider that the activity is solely in line. This means that the turnover that would be associated with that activity would be aligned with the taxonomy objectives. For example, if this is 10% of the turnover of a company, we would consider that 10% of the turnover of that company is taxonomy aligned.

Taxonomy and the Financial Sector

How will that information be used is part of the Sustainable Finance Action Plan, that is because the big first users of this data are the operators in the financial sector. The financial products like the investment funds, the insurance portfolios, the discretionary mandate, the pension funds, all of those that have claimed to have objectives as far as delivering a positive environmental impact are required to report by the 1st of January 2012. Operators have to set what is their ambition in terms of what is the minimum percentage of the portfolio that will be invested in economic activities that are being considered as aligned and then, annually, to report the percentage of alignment.

This is really a big shift in terms of data quantification in the field because, for once, there is a set of rules that will be universally applied across Europe and quantified in a comparable way between different financial products.

Of course, for the portfolio to be in a position to calculate this data, the financial operators need to have the data from the underlying companies. That is why companies doing non-financial reporting will also be required, at least in Europe, to publish their percentage of alignment with the six environmental objectives of the taxonomy and Key Performance Indicators (KPIs). All this to be able to determine what is the weight of the sustainable activity in the company. It could be per turnover if it is an operational activity per CapEx if it is a transition plan, or Operational Expenditure (OpEx).

The implementation of the regulation strarted fast, the first part in January 2022 and the second part in January 2023.

An important step to understand the way the taxonomy will be used is that not only non-financial corporates will be required to report on the taxonomy alignment but also financial undertakings that report on them. There will be banks, insurance companies, and large asset managers required to publish the taxonomy alignment ratio.

The rules on how this will be calculated are being finalised and this is really crucial for the implementation because that means that a bank will be required to publish its green asset ratio: the percentage of its investment but also lending activities or commissions generated from activities that are aligned with the taxonomy.

In a way, if a bank wants to report a higher green asset ratio, it will be incentivised, in fact, to lend to companies that can demonstrate their alignment with the taxonomy.

INNOVATIONS IN SUSTAINABLE REPORTING: A CHALLENGING EVOLUTION TOWARDS THE FUTURE

The Reporting System

In the corporate information system, which is necessary for internal management but also to inform investors, researchers, policy-makers, and the general public on business activity, the 'reporting system' plays a critical role. This is a specific framework for transparency and disclosure of information; in other words, it is a process of making fats and possibly quality data known to the public.

Note that 'sustainability' is not just about reporting on the past or what has happened. When we are reporting on sustainability, we need to include risk analysis and future goals, *i.e.* targets to enhance the positive impact on the environment and society.

With sustainable development, companies are building a new business structure, in a changed working environment, and therefore they are including sustainability in the strategy and at the core of the businesses. The reporting system is functional for all of this.

The EU Legislation

In the EU, the directive on 'Disclosure of non-financial and diversity information by certain large undertakings and group' (Directive 2014/95/EU), which came into force in 2016, is the main driver for businesses to report beyond financial resources (EU, 2014). The directive amended the accounting directive in 2013 and introduced a new sustainability reporting from the corporate side.

The EU legislation is the result of a growing demand for impact analysis with accounting in addition to financial analysis. If we look at the directive, the reporting obligations for companies are quite high and cover environmental, social, and human rights matters, the anti-corruption fight, and bribery issues.

Companies should also report on implemented policies and results, due diligence, principal risk, and Key Performance Indicators (KPIs). They should report on relevant KPIs for business drivers, the development position, and the impact. The business model is very important for companies and they look at the key performance indicators and choose the relevant ones.

The aim of the legislation, as in the case of financial reporting where we like to see whether a company has experienced a loss or gain, is to highlight non-financial results. We would like to know whether the company has a negative impact on the environment and also on society. We would also like to see what actions the company is taking to react positively in this matter.

The Developments in the EU and at the Global Level

In the accounting practical application, when the European directive came out, they were referring to over 20 frameworks and standards that companies could use to report on non-financials.

It has been quite confusing for companies, at least in the beginning, which one they should follow and its development was really challenging. But the European Union also put forward a guidance on key reporting principles and many companies are now following this.

The experience is that many companies started reporting on non-financial, beginning from those that are obliged to follow this directive: big businesses, listed companies, public interest companies, banks, and insurance companies. We see that their reporting is improving over the years fulfilling the legislation.

A global survey made by KPMG 2020 says that over 96% of the world's largest, 250 companies are reporting on sustainability, performance and as well, 80% of companies out of 5200 of the largest 100 firms in 58 countries, are also reporting (KPMG, 2020).

The most commonly used framework in the world is the Global Reporting Initiative Standard (GRI), which is actually the only sustainable reporting framework that can demonstrate widespread global adoption. That is the framework that has been used by most of the (actually 73% of the 250) companies.

Many companies are linking the key performance indicators to the Sustainability Development Goals (SDGs) and a different framework in the same report. Often, companies are using more than one framework. They are using frameworks that are focused on environmental, social, and governance issues. They are exploring the grey area framework and the SDGs. Some are even using the UN Global Compact.

This is what companies are doing and reporting. They are working on having digitized, transparent information that they update on a regular basis, just similar to financial bookkeeping, both for the environmental and social aspects of the business.

The Present Achievements and the Future

Non-financial reporting is becoming “mainstream”, the investors are looking at and evaluating beyond financial outcomes.

From the reports, we can see that there are some of them very good with transparent and trusted information. Some others are only fulfilling the legislation, so there is a lot of work to do.

Many companies are following some frameworks and not really analysing what key performance indicators are the most important, related to their motives. For example, a bank should report more on responsible investment than maybe on the operation itself, even though that is also important, in the same waycompanies are reporting on it.

Furthermore, we see that at the company level, it is difficult to compare reports. It is also a kind of difficult to track the information for trust and transparency. Anyway, it takes time to implement this all and it is increasingly evident that companies are becoming better and better in reporting.

Hence the quality is of concern. Some companies report only on positive aspects and some companies also 'cherry pick' the KPIs. This raises a concern about 'greenwashing'. We just have to face the fact that it is a concern and it happens. There is room for improvement, transparency, and the publication of trusted information that shows both negative and positive impacts.

CONCLUSION

In this chapter, we presented the European legislation on taxonomy and non-financial reporting.

In a nutshell, the objective of the European taxonomy is today recognised, although in the US or Asia, it is also being looked at as being due and as the goal applied in other parts of the world.

Potentially, it could become an internationally recognised set of rules, which are scientifically based and, as much as possible, objective with quantified criteria to define when an activity is environmentally aligned, leading to an alignment ratio at the level of a company but also at the level of a portfolio or even more at the financial sector as a whole in the economy.

About reporting, it is very important to have a global or at least European framework. In 2022, the EU approved a Corporate Sustainability Reporting Directive (CSRD), which would amend the existing reporting requirements of the non-financial reporting directive. This was towards an improvement in EU legislation in this area.

What we expect next is that this new legislation lays the foundation for a sustainability reporting framework. Significant improvements in the first half of 2022 and the first set of standards were adopted by the end of the same year, with new requirements starting to apply, at least in part, for report purposes in 2024 covering the financial year 2023. The hope is that we could see the full disclosure required at least in January 2026 so as to be able to have trusted and transparent information in terms of sustainability reporting from companies.

The "Green Deal" and the "EU Taxonomy" are part of all this reporting from the companies, as the sustainability financial disclosure applied in EU MSs in 2021. So, companies really should include all the information relevant to their business model in the report.

This is a good direction for EU legislation that a new standard or framework is being worked on. The proposal is that they like to extend the scope to all large companies and all companies that are listed on a regulated market, including listed micro-enterprises. They would also require the audit assurance of reported information and introduce more detailed reporting requirements. The requirement to report according to mandatory EU sustainability reporting standards will also ask companies to digitally tag the reported information so it is machine-readable and fits into the European single access point as in the Capital Market Union Action Plan.

We believe this is the direction, all merging into one sustainability report: the "sustainability annual report". Then, maybe we will see the reporting of the main information in a report that is easy to read for the investors and all the stakeholders, who need to have this information.

In conclusion, there is a huge need to educate and motivate, build awareness, and involve stakeholders, to collect the relevant data to be able to publish trustworthy, a transparent information. This means also changing our-self, and changing the way we work on a daily basis.

There is still a lot of work needed to do to achieve the objectives of the EU legislation, but we see that many companies are coming very fast.

PART II: Developments in the Sub-Systems of the National-Regional Accounts and the Related Satellite Accounts for Sustainable Development Policy Purposes

CHAPTER 3

The Central Framework of National Accounts and the Satellite Accounts in A Systemic Approach to Organize Statistical Data

Edoardo Pizzoli[1,*]

[1] *Department of Finance, University of Luxembourg, Luxembourg, Luxembourg*

Abstract: The UN System of National Accounts (SNA) and the European System of Accounts (ESA) both provide a sequence of accounts, at the national and possibly regional level, describing economic activity in an accounting year. This is the core of the system of accounts which has been consolidated over several decades of implementation in official statistical offices after periodical revisions. The central framework has been progressively expanded and integrated with further accounts, to focus on specific sectors of economic activity, sub-populations of national producers, or new areas of policy interest, going far beyond the consolidated representation of the economy and society.

Today, there is a broad consensus among academia, statisticians, and experts in the field that the system of accounts should cover information on key sustainability topics. This implies including measurements of the other two dimensions of sustainability: the social and the environmental. Probably in the future, there will be a refocusing on what should be considered 'central' to this accounting framework.

Keywords: National accounts, Satellite accounts, Systemic approach, Social and environmental sustainability, Sustainable development.

INTRODUCTION

The system of national accounts provides a powerful statistical framework to describe at the macro-level the development process of an economy in a reference accounting year. The UN System of National Accounts (SNA) and the European System of Accounts (ESA) both provide the methodological basis and the sequence of economic accounts at national and possibly regional levels (UNSTAT, 2009; Eurostat, 2013). This is the core of the system which has been consolidated over time but also expanded and integrated with specific Satellite

* **Corresponding author Edoardo Pizzoli:** Department of Finance, University of Luxembourg, Luxembourg, Luxembourg; E-mail: edoardo.pizzoli@uni.lu

Accounts (SA), that attempt to cover the environmental and social dimensions interacting with economic development.

The three dimensions, together, are necessary to properly describe progress with respect to the sustainability of development and to enable policy decisions to be taken accounting for all existing interactions in the system.

Furthermore, what is considered 'central' in the framework of the system of accounts is evolving based on methodological developments, new data availability, and changing policy instruments.

After a brief consideration of the systemic approach to accounting, the methodological indications of SNA and ESA manuals are summarized with respect to the SA relevant to analyse "sustainability". The potential advantages and limitations of this statistical tool are reported at the end.

THE SYSTEMIC APPROACH TO DATA ORGANIZATION

Modern system theory, widely used in science, provides a useful approach for the analysis of sustainability applied to social issues in the broad sense, that is including economics and its natural environment (Dyball *et al.*, 2015). Extensions, such as those of chaos theory, allowed also us to consider the complexity of dynamics in our real world and how even small events and actions can affect the whole system (Lorenz, 1972). That is why even small values or variations in macro aggregates should be kept under great attention.

Macro-(national and regional) accounts have been developed following this systemic approach within the SNA and ESA (UNSTAT, 2009; EU, 2013). As mentioned, this is the proper way to describe the complex phenomenon composed of many 'parts' interacting with each other, in particular macroeconomic developments within the environmental and social spheres, even if this has to be expressed only in monetary terms. The SNA/ESA framework is structured in a central set and several satellite sets of accounts, with connected entries that consider feedback effects. This is a typical "application of a systematic accounting approach" (ESA, par. 22.10).

This "accounting framework of the SNA allows economic data to be compiled and presented in a format that is designed for purposes of economic analysis, decision-making, and policymaking" (SNA, par. 1.1). The data, after the organization into accounts, are suitable for producing statistical macro-indicators to be used for the previous purposes.

Specifically, SA has to be considered in this methodological approach based on system theory.

SATELLITE ACCOUNTS IN THE SNA SYSTEM

In the SNA manual, chapter 29 is dedicated to "Satellite accounts and other extensions".

For the SNA manual "The sequence of accounts is fully integrated in large part because of the underlying rigour of the [business] accounting system" (SNA, par. 29.1) as it is "derived from the broad bookkeeping principles" (SNA, par. 3.112). That is why "SNA works with a quadruple-entry accounting system" (SNA, par. 26.17).

SNA is, for the previous reason, "integrated, economically complete and internally consistent"; moreover, despite these characteristics, "A great deal of flexibility can be applied in its implementation" in different ways (SNA, par. 29.1). Based on that, several further systems of accounts linked to the "core accounts" (SNA, par. 17.193) can be devised.

It is possible "to select a group of products or industries ...designated here as key sectors" and "to compile a complete sequence of accounts for the key sector also" (SNA, par. 29.3). This is the development of a sub-system of "key sector accounts" (SNA, par. 29.3), which is, in this case, fully included and so coherent with the central system. An example of this, provided by the manual, is "the goods and services primarily serving tourism" (SNA, par. 29.3).

Following the manual, this approach may lead to very specific choices "for example concentrating on a single agricultural crop or mineral output" (SNA, par. 29.3). This is theoretically possible, but implementation is constrained by the availability, at the time of compilation, of basic data or disaggregated statistics.

"A further and more extensive form of flexibility is that of truly satellite account", "linked to, but distinct from, the central system" (SNA, par. 29.4). Note that "each is consistent with the central system, they may not always be consistent with each other" (SNA, par. 29.4).

"There are two types of satellite accounts" (SNA, par. 29.5): "internal satellite" or extension Satellite Accounts (SA), by introducing reclassifications and extensions; "external satellite" or supplement SA, by introducing alternative concepts (SNA, par. 29.85).

In the first case, there could be "some rearrangements of central classifications and the possible introduction of complementary elements. Such satellite accounts mostly cover accounts specific to given fields such as education, tourism and environmental protection expenditures and may be seen as an extension of the key sector accounts just referred to" (SNA, par. 29.5). "Many elements shown in a satellite account are invisible in the central accounts" as "they are merged for presentation in more aggregated figures or they are only implicit components of transactions which are estimated globally" (SNA, par. 29.5). They are "extensions" "specific to given fields such as education, tourism and environmental protection expenditures" (SNA, par. 29.5).

This type of satellite account can cover social and environmental topics relevant to analysing progress on the sustainability of the development.

"The second type of satellite analysis is mainly based on concepts that are alternatives to those of the SNA" (SNA, par. 29.6) or "may add non-economic data" (SNA, par. 29.85). For example, "a different production boundary, an enlarged concept of consumption" that "may give rise to partial complementary aggregates, the purpose of which is to supplement the central system" (SNA, par. 29.6).

This second type of SA "allows experimentation with new concepts and methodologies" that are focused on specific topics of sustainability. An example "may be the role of volunteer labour in the economy" (SNA, par. 29.8) and the introduction of a different view of the economy as the "Third or Social Economy (TSE)" (UNSTAT, 2018).

As such, these accounts are a "suitable way to explore new areas in a research context" (SNA, par. 29.85), open to other scientific areas and to the introduction of theoretical innovations that can lead to the "possibility of changes in the central system itself" (SNA, par. 29.8). For example, there may be a shift of the central focus from economic growth to human well-being, since "an individual's state of well-being, or welfare, is not determined by economic factors alone (SNA, par. 1.83), or, in addition, a full consideration of the critical "link between economic data and non-monetary information" in the system of accounts (SNA, par. 29.94).

SATELLITE ACCOUNTS FOR SUSTAINABLE DEVELOPMENT

Several examples of satellite accounts are briefly described in the SNA manual which could be important for analysing the "sustainability" of the development process: "tourism satellite account and the environmental satellite account", "the health satellite account", a "fourth area covers unpaid household production activities" (SNA, par. 29.87), "accounts for water and forests ... of the main environmental satellite account SEEA" (SNA, par. 29.88), and "further satellite accounts for agricultural products" (SNA, par. 29.88).

In these and further cases "International guidelines on satellite accounts ... may eventually move towards an accepted international standard" (SNA, par. 29.88).

Furthermore, the SNA notes that there are some cases of satellite accounts where "the boundary between satellite accounts and a straightforward elaboration of the SNA ... is not clear cut" (SNA, par. 29.86). Relevant examples for our purposes are "the treatment of NPIs in chapter 23 and the informal sector in chapter 25 are satellite accounts" (SNA, par. 29.86).

Three satellite account systems are presented in greater detail in SNA, which deal with expanding areas of the economy and are related to sustainability:

- The system of "Tourism Satellite Accounts" (TSA) developed by Eurostat, OECD, World Tourism Organization (SNA, par. 29.89-29.101);
- The "System of Environmental and Economic Accounts" (SEEA), that is "the satellite for Integrated Environmental and Economic Accounts" by UN, EC, IMF, OECD, and WB (SNA, par. 29.102-29.127);
- "The System of Health Accounts (SHA) as a joint effort by the OECD, Eurostat and WHO" (SNA, par. 29.128 – 29.142).

The last section of SNA, dedicated to "unpaid household activity", "is not concerned with a normal satellite account" (SNA, par. 29.143 – 29.161) but opens the way for the subsequent development of the system to the "Third or Social Economy (TSE) sector accounts".

The TSA "is a long-established satellite account with more than 70 countries having compiled one at some stage" and a manual of international guidelines, known as the 2008 "Tourism Satellite Accounts: Recommended Methodological Framework" published by Eurostat, OECD, World Tourism Organization and UN (UNSTAT, 2010).

We know that in the modern global economy, this is a fast-growing sector of activity with a strong impact on the environment and local communities. The purpose of TSA is to analyse in detail the demand for goods and services associated with this economic activity, in turn, associated with the statistical unit of "visitors"; describe how this supply interacts with other economic activities and, in the future, possibly link it to the impact on the environment and society. Recent publications in this context by UNWTO are: Inclusive Recovery Guide – Sociocultural Impacts of Covid-19, Issue 3: Women in Tourism (UNWTO, 2021); Buddhist Tourism in Asia: Towards Sustainable Development (2000); Recommendations on Tourism and Rural Development – A Guide to Making Tourism an Effective Tool for Rural Development (UNWTO, 2000); Sports Tourism and the Sustainable Development Goals (SDGs) (UNWTO, 2019),

The SEEA Central Framework (SEEA-CF) was adopted by the UNSC in 2012, as the first international standard for environmental-economic accounting, and the official version was published in 2014 (UN, 2014). A methodological update has been undertaken recently for ecosystem accounting (see below).

"Environmental accounts aim to reflect within a framework based on the SNA the impacts of using (and sometimes using up) natural resources and the generation of residuals that pollute the air and water. They also identify specific activities undertaken to prevent or combat the environmental impacts of human activity" (SNA, par. 29.102). This is a topic where physical measurement and accounts could be linked to standard monetary ones in national accounts, "enlarging the scope of the accounting framework by adding non-monetary information, *e.g.* on pollution and environmental assets" (ESA, par. 1.41);

The recent UN publication in this field is SEEA Ecosystem Accounting (SEEA EA) (UN, 2017, 2021) which broadens the vision by adopting a spatial approach to accounting, as the benefits the society receives from ecosystems depend on the position of those assets in the landscape in relation to the beneficiaries.

Finally, Eurostat published several manuals for the SEEA implementation in EU: Environmental Protection Expenditure Accounts (EPEA) (Eurostat, 2017a), Environmental Goods and Services Sector (EGSS) (Eurostat, 2016a), Manual for air emissions accounts (Eurostat, 2015a), Resource Management Expenditure Accounts (ReMEA) – draft guidelines (Eurostat, 2014b), Physical Energy Flow Accounts (PEFA) Manual (Eurostat, 2014c), and more on specific environmental topics.

The SHA manual, A System of Health Accounts (SHA) 2011 - revised edition, was published by OECD, WHO, and the EC in 2017 (OECD *et al*, 2017).

The healthcare industry is expanding and has a particular role in relation to sustainability, as dealing with the state of the human body and mind is a key factor in well-being and the possibility of long-term development of society. The expenditure perspective is considered in SHA but, similar to the previous satellite accounts, several extensions are possible.

Lastly, there are several methodological developments focusing on households, civil society, and the non-market and non-profit economy. Several countries performed studies or produced national satellite accounts in this field. Today we find, among others, manuals on Household Production and Consumption: Proposal for a Methodology of Household Satellite Accounts (Eurostat, 2003), Beyond the Market: Designing Non-market Accounts for the United States (NRC, 2005), and Satellite Account on Non-profit and Related Institutions and Volunteer

Work that leads to the Third or Social Economy (TSE) accounts system (UNSTAT, 2018). These accounting systems combine items for the economy and society, which have been left outside the so-called production boundary in SNA together with internal information, using data already included in national accounts but hidden in the aggregates or classified differently.

The latter is a promising area for studying social, and even partially economic, resilience and sustainability. For example, "extended accounts can be drawn up which also include the imputed monetary values of, for example (a) domestic and personal services produced and consumed within the same household; (b) changes in leisure time; (c) amenities and disadvantages of urban life; (d) inequalities" (ESA, par. 1.46). Even more, considering that "Welfare has many dimensions, most of which are not best expressed in monetary terms. A better solution for measuring welfare is, therefore, to use, for each dimension, separate indicators and units of measurement. The indicators could be, for example, infant mortality, life expectancy, adult literacy, and national income per capita. These indicators could be incorporated into a satellite account." (ESA, par. 1.47).

In conclusion, but not least, further developments are expected to focus on economic issues relevant to economic sustainability, as already mentioned in the original manuals, that "depend on a combination of the evolution of economic processes (such as new financial instruments), advances in statistical estimation and measurement techniques, and improvements in data collection" (in "C - The SNA in the context of other statistical systems - Future developments: the research agenda"; UNSTAT, 2009). ESA manual also mentions satellite accounts on standard economic topics (labour, productivity and growth, R&D, balance of payments, government finance) and corporate activity (ESA, par. 22.06), but the "non-observed economy" that includes the informal sector is also very relevant in this context (ESA, par. 11.26). Finally, new developments are expected in emerging areas of globalization such as, for example, the "digital economy" and proposals for new SA are underway by the UN Advisory Expert Group on National Accounts (UN-ISWGNA) and by some pilot countries (IARIW, 2020; BEA, 2020).

In relation to economic sustainability, accounting at the corporate level is also evolving due to legislation and regulations in the EU, the US, and other countries.

LINKS BETWEEN NATIONAL AND BUSINESS ACCOUNTS

The link between macro- (aggregated) and micro- (corporate) accounts is an important step in their compilation as the latter provides the primary input for the former. SNA introduces the "links to commercial accounting" in the chapter on "Measuring corporate activity" (SNA, par. 21.60-21.66). ESA dedicates a chapter to the measurement of corporate activity and the transition from business accounts to national accounts (ESA, Chap. 21).

"Business accounts represent ... a major source of information for corporate activity in national accounts" and they "share with business accounting a number of characteristics" (ESA, par. 21.01).

"Business accounting is moving to apply shared international standards. Harmonisation at the world level began on 29 June 1973 with the creation of the International Accounting Standards Committee (IASC) whose mission was to develop basic accounting standards referred to as IAS (International Accounting Standards) and then later as IFRS (International Financial Reporting Standards), that could be applied across the world. In the European Union, the consolidated accounts of EU-listed companies are prepared according to the IFRS frame of reference from 2005 onwards" (ESA, par. 22.02).

Legislation and regulations in the EU are moving forward rapidly with specific non-financial reporting requirements, starting from large entities and groups of enterprises and the financial sector: Directive 2014/95/EU specifically on non-financial reporting (NFRD) (EU, 2014), Regulation 2088/2019 on sustainable finance disclosure (EU, 2019) and Regulation 852/2020 on taxonomy for sustainable finance (EU, 2020). In 2022, the European Commission adopted a Corporate Sustainability Reporting Directive (CSRD) with Directive 2022/2464 (EU, 2022).

Today, approximately 11700 large companies in Europe are subject to the reporting requirements of the NFRD. This means that in the coming years, national accounts will have new data for implementing satellite accounts within the area of social and environmental sustainability, as soon as definitions and forms stabilize in corporate accounting.

ADVANTAGES AND LIMITATIONS OF SATELLITE ACCOUNTS

SNA and ESA offer a chance to widen the core system by producing satellite accounts that are either internal, using data already included in national accounts but classified differently, or external, including things that are not covered in the core system but based on the same concepts and definitions. For ESA, "the central framework can be used as a building-block-system to serve many important specific data needs" developed in SA (ESA, par. 22.01).

Let us consider the main advantages and limitations of SA.

First of all, the "major advantages of satellite accounts include … application of a systematic accounting approach" (ESA par., 22.10). In the EU statistical system, "The wide range of satellite accounts illustrates that the national accounts serve as a frame of reference for a variety of statistics" (statistical frame) (ESA, par. 22.09). That is why a system of SA makes it possible to enrich macro-information on the sustainability of the development process, adopting the same accounting framework and approach consolidated in macroeconomics and economic policies.

Keeping a macro view on the "totality" of the dynamics by ensuring coherence among the different systemic representations, in terms of categories and definitions, allows the production of compatible measures and generates many synergies in terms of estimation in a complex and costly data production world.

SA is a powerful tool to get insights specifically for policy use (policy-focused), enabling us to understand the systemic links among the measured aggregates and the interacting populations of units behind them.

SA is a base for calculating indicators: "As with the SNA, the SEEA accounts provide a score-keeping function from which key indicators can be derived and a management function can be used in the analysis of policy options. The accounts provide a sound basis for the calculation of measures which may already be included in sets of sustainable development indicators, but they may also be used to develop new indicators, such as environmentally adjusted macro-aggregates which would not otherwise be available" (SNA, par. 29.104).

Furthermore, SA, specifically SEEA, allows to consider "extending the SNA to allow the effects of depletion and degradation to impact the macro-aggregates such as GDP" (extended view) (SNA, par. 29.105). This means that several feedbacks between accounting systems in different spheres can be analysed.

The limitations of SA are rooted in two main issues: the difficulty of collecting some kind of data, essential for filling SA accounts, and the methodology and the tool itself, as has been evident in its standard economic applications. It should be added that, in practical implementations of SA, these issues are compounded by the reduction of resources dedicated to SA production in National Statistical Offices (NSOs).

Specific data that is required to allow some disaggregation of main economic aggregates or to measure narrow phenomena are not recorded (due to data unavailability) or are difficult to estimate, even if, paradoxically, plenty of big data are nowadays available.

Furthermore, the processing times and disclosure of accounts are often too slow with respect to policy decision needs (statistics delay).

Even the feedback in the systems of accounts can make it difficult to "read" the registered measures and, to complicate their understanding, the latter require continuous revisions over time of the time series, which can generate uncertainty and a "perception" of unreliability (accounts readability).

Finally, oversimplification with numerical representation of the development process, especially for links to environmental and social aspects that have to be expressed in monetary terms, can lead to overly easy conclusions by non-technical readers and, ultimately, ineffective decisions by policymakers (oversimplified information).

CONCLUSION

Today, there is a broad consensus among academia and experts in the field that the SNA/ESA system of accounts should have broader coverage, especially over key "sustainability" topics and issues. This implies that social and environmental measurements should be included in the system, connected and coherent with the economic aggregates. Probably, in the future, there will be a refocus on what should be central to this accounting framework, towards well-being and sustainability (UNSTAT, 2020).

The SA systems already studied in the last decade, which focus on areas relevant to sustainable development, should be further developed and implemented in more countries to enable the production of relevant statistics that respond to present policy needs (for example: the recent European Green Deal). Further proposals for new SA are underway by UN-ISWGNA. Not all SAs have the same relevance for sustainability and some of them are becoming priorities under political pressure.

Recent developments in business accounting, particularly in the area of non-financial reporting, will allow companies to provide data that is currently unavailable, in the economic and especially environmental and social dimensions. The SA system for sustainability purposes can be improved by following the business accounting developments.

In addition, there are several side statistical benefits and limited costs in implementing SA. That is why there is a wider use today and new applications are being proposed. A criticality that remains, in common with standard accounting systems, is the timing of the final release and dissemination of data: even if it is a very effective tool, information becomes ineffective if does not arrive on time.

Statistics provides support to quantitative-based decision-making. A solution to this specific issue is expected from more efficient technology but also by an improved proportionality of the resources invested in SA production by governments. A final critical part remains on the narrow estimation of specific data and their quality control, which are necessary to compile reliable SA.

In conclusion, keeping a macro and multi-dimensional vision of the development process, as is the case with SA, is extremely important considering the nature of the issues related to "sustainability" and the high number of systemic interactions between variables and units involved.

CHAPTER 4

Natural Capital in National and Regional Accounts: The Example of India

P. Bhanumati[1,*]

[1] *National Statistical Office, New Delhi, India*

Abstract: It is now clear to countries around the world that economic development is no longer sustainable at the expense of the natural environment. Only economic accounting integrated with environmental accounting allows for controlling any imbalances and finding out the trade-offs for appropriate policy decisions. In developing countries, like India, solutions are being sought to enhance the value of natural capital in policy decisions, in a similar way as in developed economies.

This chapter introduces how India is implementing the System of Economic and Environmental Accounting (SEEA), now recognised by the UN as an international statistical standard. It also highlights new opportunities in data availability and technological advances that suggest innovative ways to exploit this information for environmental accounting purposes.

Keywords: Environmental-economic accounting, Ecosystem services, India statistics, National-regional accounts, Natural capital.

INTRODUCTION

The geographical area of the Asian subcontinent administered by the Indian government, is characterized by a great diversity of natural ecosystems: from deserts to swamps and forests, from plateaus to plains, mangroves and coral reefs, just to give some examples. Ten biogeographic zones can be distinguished along with successive variations in agro-climatic areas, ranging from the peaks of the Himalayas in northern India, through the central arid and semi-arid regions, to the tropical rainforests in the south and the coasts of the Indian Ocean (Bhanumati, 2021).

In India, the natural environment is discussed at the constitutional level in the Principal Directives of State Policy, of 1950. They indicate the commitment of the

* **Corresponding author P. Bhanumati:** National Statistical Office, New Delhi, India;
E-mail: p.bhanumati@gov.in

Edoardo Pizzoli (Ed.)

Indian state to it, specifically forests and wildlife, and impose a fundamental duty of protection and improvement on its citizens (Art. 48A and Art. 51A; Government of India, 2022). The various states address the environment through legislative and administrative instruments, considering the federal system of government of India; while the Union Parliament makes laws for the entire country (Art. 25 of the Constitution). Powers are distributed according to three lists of area (Union, State and Concurrent). For example, land and water are state matters, while forests and wildlife are concurrent matters. Environment is a concurrent subject and statistics are produced following this distribution among the various levels of government.

The Ministry of Statistics and Programme Implementation (MoSPI) of the Government of India acts as a liaison agency for the integrated planning and development of the statistical system. For environmental statistics and accounts, to provide accessibility, MoSPI has created a compendium of environmental statistics, consolidating the historical series since 1997 on the basis of the United Nations Framework for the Development of Environmental Statistics (FDES) 1984 (MoSPI, 1998-2016).

In 1997, MoSPI established a technical working group on Natural Resource Accounting (NRA) to study the introduction to the environmental accounts system. A study was undertaken in a province for the period 1999-2000 and discussed among academia and statistical offices. In order to develop a specific uniform methodology, MoSPI commissioned a series of state-level studies on natural resources: land, forests, air, water and subsoil (MoSPI, 2006; 2008). In 2011, MoSPI created an expert group, chaired by Prof. Partha Dasgupta, from the University of Cambridge in England, to develop a framework for India's green national accounts and propose a roadmap for their implementation. The report of 2013 titled "Green National Accounts in India- A Framework" (MoSPI, 2013) recommended the compilation following the United Nations System of Environmental-Economic Accounting (SEEA).

THE ENVIRONMENTAL-ECONOMIC ACCOUNTING SYSTEM

To measure growth at the regional level, several statistical indicators are used, with GDP and other macroeconomic aggregates at the core. In order to achieve sustainability, it is essential to supplement economic information with information on the state of natural capital such as biotic, and abiotic resources and the ecosystems. The natural environment provides raw materials for production and this causes dependence on environmental conditions. Further social benefits derive from being able to enjoy nature. Understanding the interdependence that exists between the environment and the economy is very important for decision-makers when they develop their growth policies, to ensure a sustainable use of natural resources.

Within the United Nations, a comprehensive, internationally agreed conceptual framework has been developed: the System of Environmental-Economic Accounting (SEEA) (UN, 2014). The objective of the SEEA accounts is to describe the environmental burden of economic activity, and the current state of the natural environment and to provide data for environmental indicators. Labour, capital, and nature interact in the national economy to enable its growth.

With these integrated accounts, a range of macro-level issues, such as the efficient use of resources and their productivity, can be studied through techniques such as decomposition analysis and structural input-output analysis. We can distinguish two main sub-systems: SEEA-Central Framework (SEEA-CF) adopted by the United Nations Statistical Commission as the international standard for environmental-economic accounting in 2012 (UN, 2014), that considers "individual environmental assets", such as land, water and energy resources, and the flows between these assets between the environment and the economy. SEEA-Ecosystem Accounting (SEEA-EA), adopted in 2021, is a coherent framework for integrating an assessment of ecosystems and ecosystem service flows with measures of economic and other human activities (UN, 2021). Both form the integrated basis of this system that can be applied to specific subject areas.

DEVELOPMENTS OF THE ACCOUNTING SYSTEM IN INDIA

MoSPI started compiling environmental accounts under the SEEA framework in 2018 to ensure international comparability. Some results have already been published in "EnviStats-India".

This publication consists of two annual issues. Volume I covers various dimensions of environmental statistics (EnviStats-India, 2019-2022a) in line with the United Nations Framework for the Development of Environmental Statistics (FDES) 2013 (UNSTAT, 2017). FDES provides indicators on the state of the environment, our dependence on it, our impact and that of the environment on human life, environmental protection and management. The publication of 2021 provides information on 222 indicators from the 2013 FDES. Volume II presents the SEEA reports that provide a systematic view of the state of the environment in India in relation to resources and ecosystems (EnviStats India, 2018; 2019-2022b). In this publication, we find ((MoSPI, 2021; Table **1**):

Table 1. SEEA accounts system in India.

Account	Topic
Ecosystem extent	Change matrix of Land Use – Land Cover (LULC) Asset Account for Land Use Land Cover (LULC) Land Degradation Account, from Wetland Extent Account
Ecosystem condition	Soil nutrient indices Water quality accounts Forest condition account Cropland condition account
Ecosystem services	Crop provisioning services (monetary) Timber provisioning services (monetary) Non-Timber Forest Products (NTFP) provisioning services (monetary) Carbon retention services provided by forests (physical and monetary) Nature-based tourism (monetary) Soil erosion prevention services provided by croplands (physical)
Thematic Accounts	Biodiversity - The extent of protected areas State-wise floral and faunal species accounts Species Richness of IUCN Red List species
Individual environmental asset accounts (SEEA CF)	Forests – Growing Stocks of Timber and Carbon Water

A major contribution to the development of these accounts in India has been made by the project "Natural Capital Accounting and Valuation of Ecosystem Services (NCAVES)", supported by the European Union, with the collaboration of UNSD, UNEP, Secretariat of CBD and other national partners. This project was led by MoSPI along with the Ministry of Environment, Forests and Climate Change, the National Remote Sensing Centre and other government agencies (MoSPI, 2021). A first pilot study was performed by the Indian Institute of Science in Bengaluru, in the Indian state of Karnataka. Ecosystem accounts and condition indicators for a set of ecosystem services have been developed. With scenario analysis, it was possible to evaluate land use, conservation, reforestation and landscape policies. Furthermore, a tool, the India - Environmental Valuation Look-up (India-EVL), was allowed access to data and a series of evaluation studies from 2000 assessed the quality and applicability of policies, in particular in the context of value transfer.

Alongside MoSPI, the office of the comptroller and auditor general of India also compiles accounts of revenue and expenditure in the exploitation of natural resources and related activities (GASAB, 2020). These accounts allow to link SEEA with SNA (Bhanumati, 2021).

DATA AVAILABILITY AND POSSIBLE DEVELOPMENTS

The development of environmental accounts, due to their spatial dimension, requires resources and investments in new data sources. It is also essential to integrate traditional statistical sources with administrative and remote sensing ones.

NSO India has also started this process thanks to the data from the Indian space program integrated with those available from USGS and ESA. Furthermore, the InVEST suite, developed by Stanford University with other international institutions (University of Minnesota, Chinese Academy of Sciences, The Nature Conservancy World Wildlife Fund and Stockholm Resilience Centre), has been used to understand the dispersion of nature-based tourism service values across the country (InVEST, 2022).

Another emerging source of environmental data is new corporate reporting. In India, the philosophy of responsible business was introduced in the National Voluntary Guidelines on social, environmental and economic responsibilities of business (NVG), 2011 (Government of India, 2011) and subsequently incorporated into the Companies Act, 2013 as the National Guidelines for Responsible Business Conduct (NGRBC) in 2019 (Government of India, 2019). These guidelines envisage a broader responsibility of a company towards its stakeholders beyond the interests of its shareholders: its employees, the community and, for our purposes, the natural environment.

The top 1000 companies in terms of market capitalization in India are required to file a Business Responsibility and Sustainability Report (BRSR) following the guidelines (Bhanumati, 2021). The prescribed BRSR format requires reporting the dependence on natural capital, energy, and water consumption, as well as waste management, wastewater and air emissions.

Listed entities are encouraged to produce this report including environmental information as well (SEBI, 2020). Other companies in India are already compiling sustainability reports voluntarily along with financial information (WBSCD, 2018). This information is useful to companies to identify and assess their direct and indirect impacts on the environment and their dependence on natural capital. Studies by industry associations highlight the need for environmental conservation and restoration to ensure sustainable growth of their business sectors (CII-ITC, 2020; FICCI, 2014).

This process of developing the environment with business reporting is ongoing and will take time to be fully integrated into the SEEA accounts.

CONCLUSION

In India, there is a growing awareness that achieving development goals requires taking the environment and its natural resources into account.

Data and statistical production are rapidly adapting to the new policy needs and environmental accounts are a robust multi-purpose information system suitable for assessing sustainability.

Today, SEEA-compliant accounts present comparable information, based on standard definitions and a robust conceptual framework. Furthermore, the need for their compilation, is encouraging the investment in new comprehensive and coherent databases. reports and analyses.

CHAPTER 5

Non-Profit Sector Accounting in the Italian Official Statistics

Massimo Lori[1] and **Chiara Orsini**[1,*]

[1] *Department for Statistical Production, ISTAT, Rome, Italy*

Abstract: The implementation of the United Nations 2030 agenda for sustainable development requires a solid statistical framework that has prompted the National Institutes of Statistics (NISs) to produce Sustainable Development Goals (SDGs) indicators. While nonprofit institutions and social entrepreneurship are increasingly recognized as important actors supporting the achievement of sustainable development goals (Salamon *et al.*, 2015), official statistics investigating those actors are rare. Even in the absence of international regulations as a legal basis for producing social economy and the third sector-related statistics, the Italian Institute of Statistics (ISTAT) has been producing official statistics on the core characteristics of NonProfit Institutions (NPIs) for more than 20 years (definition in S.15; Eurostat, 2013).

The objective of this chapter is to show the state of the art of statistical production on the non-profit sector and Corporate Social Responsability (CRS) in Italy. With the objective of enhancing the available information and expanding the perspective of social economy, the ISTAT permanent census of enterprises has investigated the corporate Environmental, Social, and Governance (ESG) performance, including corporate social CSR. Undeniably, the integration of data sources, combining survey results with administrative data, positively contributes to acquiring insight into SDGs while enhancing measures and statistics on the third sector and social economy, such as the creation of a satellite account of NPIs (UNSTAT, 2018).

Keywords: Corporate and social responsibility, Non-profit sector accounting, Social economy, Third sector statistics.

INTRODUCTION

In the last decades, the interest of statisticians, policymakers, and social scientists has been focusing on organizations that are different from market firms or public

* **Corresponding author Chiara Orsini:** Department for Statistical Production, ISTAT, Rome, Italy;
E-mail: chorsini@istat.it

Edoardo Pizzoli (Ed.)

agencies. In literature and public debate, this type of social institution is differently mentioned as “non-profit”, “voluntary”, “civil society”, or “third sector” organizations, and commonly these terms also include sports and recreation clubs, art and cultural associations, private schools, research institutes, hospitals, charities, religious institutions, social services organizations, advocacy groups, and charitable foundations.

The reasons for this interest in those organizations, named “nonprofit institutions” (NPIs), are to find not only the functional importance assumed in the context of social policy and the legal framework but also in their specific way of doing business and in interpreting economic action. In brief, we can identify four reasons behind the public interest:

- NPIs economic relevance has been growing in countries throughout the world. Despite the idea of the nonprofit sector's marginality in contemporary societies, the empirical evidence has shown the economic growth of this sector even in recent periods of economic crisis and the capabilities to solve persistent social and economic issues;
- NPIs are increasingly concerned with public policy. Against the backdrop of the welfare state crisis, a process of “non-profitization” of social policies is taking place as governments increasingly give to nonprofit organizations public services (Salamon, 2016);
- NPIs have distinct organizational behaviour and features that differentiate them from other economic sectors. At least for some analytical purpose, it is important to split NPIs out from other economic actors, considering their specific organizational structure and social functions;
- NPIs’ role is to promote democracy, pluralism and social cohesion. A more accurate representation of the nonprofit sector appears even more crucial if we consider the social and economic relevance. Indeed, NPIS can play a fundamental part in the construction and maintenance of a vibrant and cohesive society.

Therefore, in recent years, the need for statistical information on the non-profit sector without privileging only the world of business firms and public agencies has increased.

The chapter explores, thus, how and to what extent the Italian Institute of Statistics (ISTAT) is committed to producing official statistics of the nonprofit sector, in order to investigate emerging issues.

NONPROFIT SECTOR IN THE OFFICIAL STATISTICS

The measurement of the nonprofit sector has always challenged scholars and organizations dealing with official statistics. In fact, nonprofit institutions are not always easily identifiable, particularly when there is no legal framework to identify them when they are not legally formalized. Nonetheless, the international regulations concerning the production of official statistics provide some definitions, identifying the characteristics that distinguish nonprofit institutions. A general definition of nonprofit institutions, applicable to different national contexts, is contained in the System of National Accounts (UNSTAT, 2009: 61, 455) which states that:

"Non-profit institutions (NPIs) are legal or social entities created for the purpose of producing goods and services but whose status does not permit them to be a source of income, profit or other financial gains for the units that establish, control or finance them [...]. The distinguishing feature that identifies an NPI is that its status does not permit it to be a source of income, profit, or other financial gains for the units that establish, control, or finance it. An NPI may make a profit, it may be exempted from taxes, and it may have a charitable purpose but none of these are determining characteristics. The only essential criterion for a unit to be treated as an NPI is that it may not be a source of income, profit or financial gain to its owners".

Therefore, NPIs can produce goods and services for sale like for-profit businesses. However, the above-mentioned definition states that none of these characteristics distinguish NPIs from other institutional units considered in national accounts. There is only one decisive character: the constraint of non-distribution of profits. For an organization to be classified as a nonprofit institution must not be a source of income, profit, or other financial gains for those who set up, control, or finance them (businesses, public administrations, families or individuals, *etc.*).

However, this definition does not provide a comprehensive classification of the contribution of nonprofit institutions in the 4 sub-sectors of the economy in the SNA (Non-financial corporations, S11; Financial corporations, S12; General government, S13; Households sector, S15). Moreover, the contribution of the nonprofit sector to the economy results underestimated and its characterization, is biased, if the contribution is assigned to other sub-sectors. Indeed, the primary objective of SNA 2008 and ESA 2010 is to determine the criteria for the allocation of NPIs to the appropriate institutional sectors of SNA, *i.e.*, government and financial and non-financial corporation sectors. Regarding the remaining NPIs serving the household sector, a separate sector, *i.e.* Non-Profit Institutions Serving Households (NPISHs), is created for the purpose of distinguishing the revenues and final consumption expenditures of households, as distinct from those of NPIs (UNSTAT, 2003). Therefore, NPIs are taken into account by SNA 2008 and ESA 2010 but they are not grouped into a specific economic sector. Although NPIs reflect important economic, social, and political dimensions, the Nonprofit sector is not well represented and identified by the framework of the System of National Accounts. Thus, SNA does not provide a comprehensive statistical picture of NPIs, dealing with the classification of NPIs to the institutional sectors based on certain characteristics that NPIs share with other units assigned to those sectors.

An important contribution to establishing exhaustive identification and coverage of the nonprofit sector came from the publication of the Handbook on Non-profit Institutions in the Framework of National Accounts (UNSTAT, 2003) and the updated version (UNSTAT, 2018). The UN Handbook carefully defines what belongs to a "non-profit institution", the activities carried out and the products/services it produces/delivers, and the accounting and financial items. From a statistical point of view, the key element is the definition of the constitutive characteristics of the institutional units called "nonprofit". According to the operational definition recommended in the Handbook (UNSTAT, 2003, p.18), the constitutive elements of a nonprofit institution are five:

The non-profit sector consists of units that are: (a) Organizations; (b) Not-for-profit and non-profit-distributing; (c) Institutionally separate from government; (d) Self-governing; (e) Non-compulsory.

From an operational point of view, the UN Handbook listed important aspects, especially for the purposes of measurement, which aims to economically characterize the units in the sector. Therefore, it is stated that NPIs must:

- Have a stable and formal organization;
- To be able to register cash accounts and balance sheets;
- Not pursue profit as their main mission and cannot distribute it;
- Be private or institutionally separated from public administrations;
- Finally, participation in their activities must be (to some extent) voluntary.

Furthermore, the Handbook has introduced a specific classification International Classification of Non-profit Organizations (ICNPO) to classify the activities performed by nonprofit institutions. The ICNPO classification is more relevant than the Nomenclature of Economic Activities (NACE) for describing the typical activities of NPIs that in many cases are not highlighted in the NACE scheme. In 2018, the ICNPO was updated when the Handbook (UNSTAT, 2018) was revised (and now includes a broader set of third-sector organization activities within the nonprofit sector).

SUSTAINABLE DEVELOPMENT GOALS

Nonprofit institutions and social entrepreneurship are increasingly recognized as important actors supporting the achievement of sustainable development goals (Salamon *et al.*, 2015). The NPIs' contribution to social well-being and sustainable development can be found in: the way of being (as places of active participation), the way they operate (they create networks and relationships among individuals), and the issues they deal with (care for people in conditions of fragility or protection of the commons) (*Forum Terzo Settore*, 2017). The "outcome" of nonprofit institutions is the creation of trust and social capital (Putnam *et al.*, 1993). NPIs perform a crucial social function: they create conditions and opportunities for active participation for citizens and they encourage inclusive processes. In addition, NPIs create the so-called "positive externalities", having a social function. The production system generates social costs (called "negative externalities"): from land consumption to environmental damage, social tensions or fractures (insider *Vs* outsider), till the consumption of relational goods, and capital social. The Sustainable Development Goals (SDGs), approved by the United Nations in 2015, design an inclusive development model, where many principles and values are pursued by the nonprofit sector. In fact, considering the ICNPO, it is possible to note that every activity carried out by nonprofit institutions can be linked to several SDGs (Table **1**).

Table 1. ICNPO activity and related sustainable development goals.

Type of Activity	SDGs
Income support and maintenance	1
International activities/humanitarian aid and external aid for economic development	1, 2, 5, 6,10
Economic, social and community development	1, 5, 7, 8, 9, 10, 11, 12
Sports	3
Hospitals and rehabilitation	3
Nursing homes	3
Mental health and crisis intervention	3
Other health services	3
Social services	3
Culture and arts	4
Primary and secondary education	4
Higher education	4
Other education	4, 8
Civic and advocacy organizations	5, 12, 16

(Table 1) cont.....

Type of Activity	SDGs
Employment and training	8
Research	9
Other recreation and social clubs	11
Emergency and relief	11
Housing	11
Animal protection	13, 14, 15
Development and housing	14, 15
Law and legal services	16

Source: (*Forum Terzo Settore*, 2017).

ISTAT Commitment on NPIs Official Statistics

ISTAT's strategy to measure the economic contribution and social impact of the nonprofit sector has been built over the last two decades. The production of official statistics regarding the nonprofit sector was launched in the nineties in Italy. In 1991, the 7th General Census of Industry and Services provided for the first time an overview of "non-commercial institutions" in Italy, by disseminating the core statistical information such as the number of institutions, the dimension of human resources (employees and volunteers) employed as well as the economic activities (ISTAT, 1995). Subsequently, since 1996, several surveys have been conducted on specific typologies of nonprofit institutions such as the voluntary organizations listed in the regional registers (Italian Law on Volunteering L. 266/91), social cooperatives, and the foundations surveyed.

In the last decade, numerous studies have provided further insight into the nonprofit sector, due to its increasing importance in the economic system. Nonprofit institutions are considered as leading actors not only in terms of employment and economic dimensions, but also in terms of social value, social capital, and its impact on individual and collective well-being. However, the shortage of comprehensive approaches in producing high-quality, relevant, and timely data on the nonprofit area has affected scientific research regarding NPIs socio-economic impact, as well as policy-making process. At the international level, the lack of harmonized statistical standards, definitions, and methodologies impeded to provide a complete picture of the economic weight of non-profit institutions across countries.

To respond to the growing interest of, statisticians, policymakers, and social scientists, in the early to mid-1990s, ISTAT, took part in the Johns Hopkins Comparative Nonprofit Sector Project (CNP), The research project aims to define the scope, structure, financing, and the role of the private nonprofit sector in several countries, led by the Center for Civil Society Studies at the Johns Hopkins University (JHU CCSS). The objective of the project is to provide a comparative empirical approach, a common framework and set of definitions, as well as a global information-gathering strategy to evaluate the impact of these organizations and their contributions, as well as the drawbacks they entail. The CNP provided a nonprofit institution definition, classification of economic activities carried out, and a set of dimensions to explain the sector size, composition, character, and the role linked to history, legal arrangements, religious backgrounds, cultures, socioeconomic structures, and patterns of government policy.

In this context, the United Nations together with the contributions from SNA experts, national accountants, and other specialists from a variety of developed and developing countries developed statistical standards and guidelines for the development of data on Non-Profit Institutions (NPIs), the Handbook on Nonprofit Institutions in the System National Accounts. By adopting the UN definition and approach, ISTAT conducted the First Census of Private Institutions and Nonprofit Enterprises in 2000. The census provided the first official statistical overview of the nonprofit sector in Italy and the main dimensions, internationally comparable. In line with the UN classification and definition, ISTAT was the forefront and pioneer in producing official statistics on the nonprofit sector.

Afterward, ISTAT conducted the census of nonprofit institutions within the General Census of Industry and Services in 2001 and 2011, ensuring a consistent set of information in time series. Particularly, the 2011 Nonprofit Institutions Census introduced significant innovations. A basic list of nonprofit institutions was created from administrative data and statistical archives, containing core information, as well as the questionnaire was enriched with thematic sections, investigating economic and social dimensions.

Moreover, the nonprofit census surveys collect information on volunteers engaging in NPIs. The definition of a volunteer adopted was in line with the International Labour Organisation (ILO) Manual of the measurement of volunteer work (ILO, 2011) as well as the multipurpose survey named 'Aspect of daily life', which also investigated social participation in Italy.

The Permanent Census: Register of Nonprofit Institutions

In line with ISTAT's "modernization strategy", stating that 'the production process is focused on the use of statistical registers, derived from administrative sources with continuous supplying mechanisms to collect information', in 2016, ISTAT implemented the permanent Census (ISTAT, 2016). Following the European Statistical System (ESS) Vision 2020 principle in strengthening the use of administrative data while reducing the overall costs and burden, ISTAT has implemented the permanent census strategy, involving in this process economic units such as enterprises, public and nonprofit institutions (ESS, 2014). Unlike the traditional census, held every ten years, the economic permanent census is conducted by creating yearly the register of economic units as well as by conducting periodic surveys. This process of data integration increases the quantity and quality of the data output, by continually providing updated data on the structural characteristics to economic units through the register as well as by collecting periodic information on thematic topics through the survey. Hence, the Permanent Census of Nonprofit Institutions leads ISTAT to produce relevant annual data on the structural characteristics of nonprofit institutions, gathered through different administrative sources. Those data are integrated with periodic sample surveys, investigating social and economic dimensions as well as thematic issues of Italian nonprofit institutions.

In compliance with the international framework, ISTAT identifies NPIs following the SNA definition, which states that NPIs are "legal or social entities created for the purpose of producing goods and services but whose status does not permit them to be a source of income, profit or other financial gain for the units that establish, control or finance them" (UNSTAT, 2009, paras. 4.8 and 4.83).

In 2016, ISTAT implemented the First Permanent Census of Nonprofit Institutions (NPIs), which integrates the information gathered from the sample surveys and data from the statistical business register. The Census of Nonprofit Institutions aims to:

- Update and achieve consistency of information regarding the nonprofit sector in Italy with its economic and social dimensions;
- Gather information about organizational characteristics through a series of thematic sections, while ensuring the time series data;
- Meet the national and international informational needs by realizing the Nonprofit Satellite Account;
- Build a system of statistics comparable at the international level according to the Handbook (UNSTAT, 2003);
- Increase the availability of information in the administrative data archives;
- Realize a statistical business register of nonprofit institutions, based on the integration of administrative sources and statistical surveys and interoperable with other business registers.

Within the permanent Census framework, ISTAT created yearly the register of nonprofit institutions updated through a process of integration of administrative and statistical sources and its regular maintenance ensures the updating of the active units, providing an official source of data for statistical analysis of the nonprofit sector and its demography. Despite their diverse organizational or legal forms, the NPIs included in the register are identified, by considering the five features recommended by the UN Handbook, which together make up the operational definition of NPI institutions: Organization, Self-governing, Non-compulsory, Significant limitations on the distribution of surplus (profits), and Private (UNSTAT, 2018). Therefore, this operational definition identifies not only nonprofit institutions to be considered as NPISH but also those classified in the other institutional sectors of the system of national accounts. The NPIs Register provides identification (fiscal code, name, address, and municipality) and stratification (main economic activity, size, legal form, date of creation and date of cessation, turnover) variables. The Register contains data on the individual (workers' characteristics such as sex, age, education, nationality, *etc.*) and the main job variables (professional status, type of contract, *etc.*) by job categories. Particularly, employment is formed by internal employees and self-employed people, and so-called external workers of an enterprise which represent all people who, although not classified as employees or self-employment participate in the productive process of the enterprise on the basis of a contract. The group of external workers contains those temporary workers, used by a temporary employment agency. Employment is measured both in terms of the yearly average of job positions (computed on the basis of the weekly presence of workers) and the number of workers employed at the end of the year. The implementation process of the register has addressed two methodological issues: the identification of the statistical units and the estimate of active institutions. With respect to the first issue, Italian nonprofit institutions have a variety of legal and organizational forms (cooperatives, mutual aid societies, voluntary associations, foundations, *etc.*) due to a fragmented regulatory framework, therefore, it is necessary to integrate several administrative archives and sources to identify them. With regard to the second methodological issue, the presence of administrative sources does not guarantee nonprofit institutions' existence or activity, thus a statistical model has been implemented to distinguish active institutions from non-operating institutions. In 2020, ISTAT released the statistical data of the register of nonprofit institutions in the reference year of 2018 (ISTAT, 2014-2022).

Furthermore, in the framework of the permanent census, ISTAT periodically conducts a sample survey of nonprofit institutions, which intends to provide an overview of the nonprofit sector in Italy comparable over time, at the local level, by directly collecting data on thematic issues, such economic dimensions, the service provided, social exclusion, networking, communication and fundraising. Particularly, in 2016, ISTAT conducted a survey involving a sample of about 43 thousand nonprofit institutions. The questionnaire has been realized by a Scientific Committee composed of internal personnel, focused on national accounts and business statistics, as well as external experts such as academic scholars, experts, and relevant stakeholders, in order to meet the emerging needs and priorities of users. The main results released provided information on active nonprofit institutions in the reference year of 2015, by disseminating data on human resources (volunteers and external workers), economic resources (balance sheet and type of funding), activities (prevalent activities and services provided), vulnerability (type of vulnerable person categories), networking (type of stakeholders and type of participation), communication: (communication tools and products), and fundraising (type of fundraising carried out). Ensuring coherence with a previous permanent census, ISTAT has been planning the new sample survey of nonprofit institutions in 2022, the reference year is 2021. The 2021 survey on nonprofit institutions investigates core information on the nonprofit sector, ensuring time series, as well as emerging issues such as digitalization and resilience of nonprofit institutions after COVID-19.

MAIN DATA ON NONPROFIT SECTOR

The distribution of nonprofit institutions at the regional level is highly concentrated, with over 50% in the North, while 27.1% of the nonprofit institutions are located in the South of Italy (Table **2**). However, in the South, the trend of nonprofit institutions has been growing: since 2017, the number of institutions per 10 thousand inhabitants reached 50.7 (48.3 in 2017) in the islands and 45.7 in the South (43.7 in 2017).

Table 2. Nonprofit institutions and employees by region. year 2018, absolute values and percentage.

Region	Institutions		Employees		Volunteers (2015)
	Absolute Value	For 10,000 Inhabitants	Absolute Value	For 10,000 Inhabitants	Absolute Value
North-West	100,375	62.4	288,488	181.4	1,662,178
North-East	81,921	70.3	204,563	175.5	1,422,089
Centre	79,780	66.4	193,689	161.2	1,266,461
South	63,809	45.7	103,729	74.3	768,406
Islands	33,689	50.7	63,007	94.9	409,625
Italy	359,574	59.6	853,476	141.4	5,528,760

Source: ISTAT

In terms of local distribution, the workers and volunteers of the nonprofit institutions are employed in the North: over 55%. Considering 2017 and 2018, the number of workers employed in nonprofit institutions increased in the North (+2.6%) and the South (+1.4%) while it decreased in the Islands (-1.2%).

Although over 70 percent of employees are female, nonprofit managers are mainly male.

In terms of the legal form, the association is the most widespread (85.0%), followed by other legal forms (religious entities, sports clubs, mutual and social enterprises) (8.4%), social cooperatives (4,4%) and foundations (2.2%). The distribution per legal form shows 53.0% of workers employed in social cooperatives, 19.2% in the associations, and 12.2% in the foundations. The workers significantly increased in social cooperatives (+2.4%) and foundations (+1.9%), while they decreased in number in the associations (-3.0%).

The distribution of nonprofit institutions by economic activity is focused on cultural, sports, and recreational activities, reaching 64.4% of the institutions, followed by social services and civil protection (9.3%), Business and professional associations, unions activities (6.5%), Religion (4.7%), Education and research (3.9%) and Health (3.5%).

Paid workers are employed mainly in social services (37.3%), health (21.8%), education, and research (15.0%), development, and housing (12.0%).

In terms of human resources, 85.5% of nonprofit institutions operate without employing paid workers. However, this percentage is less than 45.0% in the development, and housing and education and research sectors. Furthermore, in these two sectors, about 20% of nonprofit institutions employ at least ten workers. On the contrary, institutions operating in the fields of culture recreation, philanthropic intermediaries, and voluntarism promotion, in most cases do not employ employees (90.0%).

Concerning the economic dimension, 61% of nonprofit institutions had income under 30 thousand euros, particularly 38.1% the income is less than 10 thousand euros and 22.6% of the nonprofit institutions were between 10 thousand and 30 thousand euros.

Whereas the medium-large nonprofit institutions (with income between 30 thousand and 100 thousand euros) were 20.9% and the large-size nonprofit institutions (with income over 100 thousand euros) were 18.4% of the total.

The main sources of revenue regarding the Italian nonprofit sector, are members' yearly contributions (27.3%), revenue from contracts and/or conventions with national and/or international public (25.1%), and revenue from selling goods and services (22.9%) (Table **3**).

Table 3. Revenues and expenditures of nonprofit sector by the type of funding source and item of expenditure, year 2015 (Million Euro).

Revenue		Expenditure
Grants and contributions free of charge from national and/or international public institutions.	2,448	Personnel expenditure.
Proceeds/revenue from contracts and/or conventions with national and/or international public.	17,661	Consultant expenditure.
Members' yearly contributions.	19,249	Refunds to volunteers.
Proceeds/revenue from selling goods and services.	16,113	Purchase of goods and services.
Contributions, gifts, donations, and bequests.	4,858	Third party contributions and funding.
Proceeds/revenue from financial assets and real estate.	5,655	Expenditure from financial assets and real estate.
Other proceeds/revenue from a private source.	4,413	Tax burden.
-	-	Other expenditures
Total	70,399	Total

Source: ISTAT

Concerning the revenue balance sheet, 85.5% of Italian nonprofit institutions receive funding from private. Only 14.5% of institutions are mainly funded by the public sector. The main items of expenditures of the nonprofit sector in Italy are the purchase of goods and services (35.2%) and personnel expenditure (32.3%).

According to ESA 2010, Nonprofit institutions provide services either at significant prices (market) or almost for free (non-market). In 2015, market producers of Nonprofit institutions were 33.2%, while non-market-oriented institutions were 66.8%, recorded in nonprofit institutions serving households. Market-oriented institutions are mainly focused on carrying out social services (12.4%), business and professional associations, unions (6.8%), education and research (6.1%), health (5.7%), and development and housing (4.8%), while non-market oriented institutions are mainly operating in the sector of culture, sports, and recreation (68.2%), religion (5.8%), law, advocacy, and politics (1.9%), environment (1.7%), international (1.5%) and philanthropic intermediaries and voluntarism promotion (1.3%).

CORPORATE SOCIAL RESPONSIBILITY (CSR)

The enterprise activities have significant impacts on social, environmental, and economic dimensions in the EU and around the world. Not just in terms of the products and services they offer or the jobs and opportunities they create, but also in terms of working conditions, human rights, health, the environment, innovation, education, and training. Integrating social, environmental, ethical, consumer, and human rights concerns into their business strategy and operations, enterprises become socially responsible. European Union and public authorities have an important role in supporting and encouraging companies to conduct their business responsibly, by introducing a set of voluntary and mandatory actions to promote Corporate Social Responsibility (CSR), while implementing the UN Guiding Principles on Business and Human Rights (UNGPs) and the UN 2030 agenda for sustainable development. Furthermore, the SDGs, particularly Goal 12 'Ensure sustainable consumption and production patterns', as well as OECD initiatives in measuring the impact of businesses on people's well-being and sustainability provide a common language and improve the quality, comparability, and coherence of information on the impact of businesses on societal progress and people's life.

In the last years, ISTAT has been exploring the impact of business decisions on sustainable development. Particularly, with the objective of enhancing the available information and expanding the perspective of social economy, ISTAT has investigated the corporate Environmental Social, and Governance (ESG) performance, including corporate social responsibility. Through combining different data sources, in 2019, ISTAT launched the Permanent Census of Enterprises, which provided a detailed picture of the Italian economic system, by integrating the data in the business register with the qualitative information, gathered by the sample survey, on emerging issues, including corporate social responsibility.

The dimensions investigated are corporate measures to increase social sustainability and working welfare, such as smart working and measures of the protection of health and safety at the workplace, as well as corporate actions linked to sustainable development, such as reducing the impact on the environment (Fig. **1**). The corporate social responsibility initiatives increase for the enterprises employing more than 250 workers, particularly considering the actions for collective interest and local development. The business strategy for sustainable development of micro-enterprises (3-9 workers) is oriented towards actions to increase working welfare, while large enterprises have more propensity to implement measures for protecting health and safety at the workplace and for reducing the impact on the environment.

Regarding corporate social responsibility, the enterprises carried out actions for the local economic development, by promoting sports activities (27.8%), humanitarian projects (24.7%), and cultural initiatives (22.2%), as well as by participating in projects to enhance social inclusion and poverty reduction (17.6%). At the regional level, the data show interesting trend differences: the enterprises located in the North of Italy are focused on sports initiatives, particularly in the Northeast, while in the South of Italy, enterprises carried out actions for reducing poverty and social exclusion. Regarding local development activities, the enterprises employing more than 250 workers are the most active in supporting local marketing strategies, through promoting the cultural heritage and protecting natural resources.

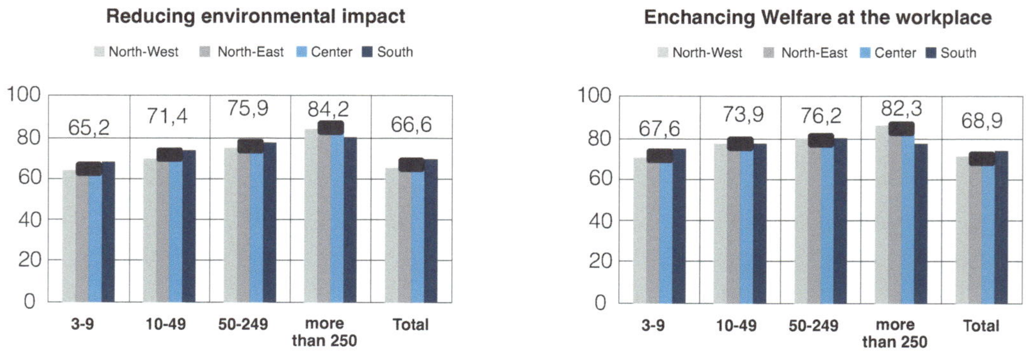

Fig. (1). Sustainable activities by class of workers and local level (Source: ISTAT).

CONCLUSION

The national account procedures ensure a consistent treatment of the actors involved in the economic system of countries. However, regarding nonprofit institutions, this approach does not represent properly the relations and the synergies between NPIs and other economic agents, which are competitors in producing goods and services (enterprises and national Government), and the final beneficiaries (households and general Government). As mentioned before, in the National Accounts, NPIs are classified into several institutional sectors having different organizational structures, sizes, and sources of revenue. Hence, the information on NPIs is spread out among the institutional sectors and, therefore associated with other types of existing institutional units.

Despite the fragmented sector, the growing interest in the dynamic and the opportunity generated by the nonprofit sector led to the creationof a satellite account for the nonprofit sector. As stated in the European Council Conclusion, 'Developing and implementing satellite accounts aim at establishing the effective contribution of the social economy to economic growth and social cohesion in the European Union' (Council of the EU, 2015). Satellite accounts are a tool to satisfy specific knowledge needs and to develop an integrated study of specific economic sectors. While remaining anchored to the core of the accounting system, the satellite accounts may adopt additional or alternative analysis definitions and categories. They are a propulsive element to enhance statistical information availability for the users and they are considered an important factor to foster future schemes in the national accounting field. A satellite account integrates the available information for NPISH units with data concerning the market NPIs and other third-sector units registered in several institutional sectors. The UN Handbook on Satellite Account on Nonprofit and Related Institutions and Volunteer Work extended the scope of the third sector, embracing a broad set of social economy organisations such as cooperatives, mutual societies, and social enterprises that meet a test of being primarily oriented to the public purpose (Fig. **2**; UNSTAT, 2018). This public purpose criterion is operationalised by the significant limitation on their distribution of profit.

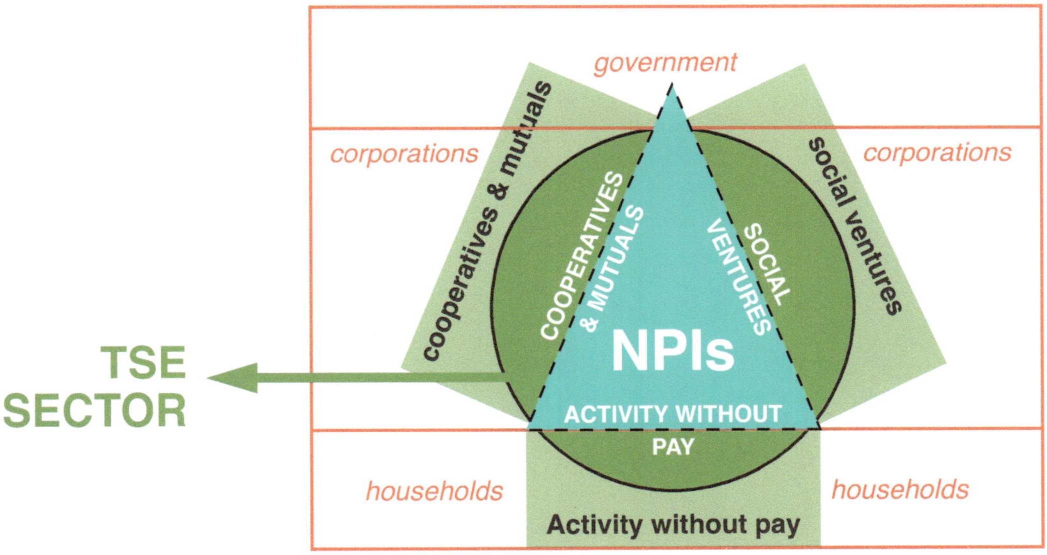

Fig. (2). The conceptualization scheme of the third or social economy (TSE) sector (Source: Salamon, 2016).

In the past two decades, Italy has progressively developed a comprehensive information system for identifying and assessing the resident NPIs in the national accounts estimation. The statistical information, provided by the census and sample surveys on the nonprofit sector, has been integrated and updated by using data from administrative sources. Through creating a system of registers in the last years, ISTAT provides information on the structure of all resident institutional units (enterprises, private and public institutions), such as size in terms of financial turnover and persons employed, legal form, and economic sector of activity. The integrated information system of Registers integrates information on the NPI structure with data on financial economic statements from administrative and fiscal sources at the micro data level. Moreover, the information on the structure, organization, control, and economic dimensions gathered by the sample survey of nonprofit institutions are combined with administrative data. The available data allowed us to implement methodologies to estimate several required variables to compile the complete set of accounts and the satellite account concepts and definitions. The current strategy planned for the NPI permanent census ensures the availability of based information and significantly enhances the quality of estimation. The system of permanent census provides a powerful integrating framework for economic statistics on the non-profit sector. A wide range of data sources are available on key dimensions of Italian nonprofit institutions, and these are planned to be combined and integrated into an SNA framework to build satellite account estimates. Comparing multiple data sources in a comprehensive and coherent accounting system will strengthen data quality and lead to the full exploitation of all available source data related to the nonprofit sector.

CHAPTER 6

An Integrated Framework for Monetary Environmental Accounts: A Pilot Study on Italy

Federica Battellini[1,*] and **Angelica Tudini**[1]

[1] *Department for Statistical Production, ISTAT, Rome, Italy*

Abstract: The research agenda of the System of Environmental-Economic Accounting–Central Framework (SEEA CF), the UN standard on environmental accounts, includes developing an integrated framework for monetary environmental accounts. At the 2017 London Group meeting, Eurostat (European Commission), leader on this topic, presented a proposal for a framework, calling, in the following year, EU member states for experimental compilation of the proposed tables. ISTAT (Italian Institute of Statistics) completed a pilot exercise in 2020, compiling the tables covered by the Eurostat layout: Supply Table, Use Table, Production account, and Expenditure account.

This chapter recalls the main accounting features of the integrated monetary framework and presents the results of the Italian pilot compilation.

Based on the same equations underlying national accounts, the integrated framework aims at assuring consistent estimates on the supply and demand of environmental products and it can be compiled starting from existing environmental accounts, EGSS mainly providing estimates on the supply of environmental goods and services, and Environmental Protection Expenditure Accounts (EPEA) providing, at present, estimates on expenditures for environmental protection purposes.

In the Italian exercise, putting EGSS and EPEA into the integrated framework layout allowed us to highlight and quantify differences in scope, coverage, and definitions between the two accounts. However, the most interesting findings concern the improvements derived from the combined use of the two accounts: the production of balanced estimates allowed for checking and adjusting inconsistencies among data, filling in gaps, and optimizing calculation processes. Furthermore, it allowed us to enlarge the supply of statistical information on the economy and the environment for Italy, beyond the present scope of EGSS and EPEA.

The exercise carried out by ISTAT is an example of how statistical information can be enhanced to better comply with the requirements of the European Green Deal and, more generally, with the demand arising from the effort towards mainstreaming environmental sustainability in all EU policies.

* **Corresponding author Federica Battellini:** Department for Statistical Production, ISTAT, Rome, Italy; E-mail: battelli@istat.it

Keywords: Environmental products classifications, Integrated framework of accounts, Monetary environmental accounts, Supply-use tables.

INTRODUCTION

The research agenda of the System of Environmental-Economic Accounting –Central Framework (SEEA CF), which is the UN "standard" on environmental accounts (UN, 2014), recognizes the need to determine whether the different aspects of monetary environmental accounts can be further integrated into a single accounting framework (Integrated Framework - IF) (Schenau, 2016).

Eurostat (European Commission), a leader on this SEEA CF research agenda topic, presented a proposal for an IF for monetary environmental accounts at the 2017 London Group meeting (Eurostat, 2017b).

The proposal is based on a common set of concepts and definitions of environmental activities, producers, and products and a set of accounting tables that can be compiled on the basis of the Environmental Goods and Services Sector account (EGSS) and Environmental Protection Expenditure Account (EPEA): Supply Table, Use Table, Environmental production account and Environmental expenditure account. The next paragraph summarizes the main features of Eurostat's IF proposal (Eurostat, 2017b, 2018), currently a work in progress and is to be finalized by the SEEA CF technical committee.

In this context, in 2020, ISTAT completed a pilot project aiming at testing an IF for monetary environmental accounts. The Eurostat's layout is the reference framework for the Italian pilot compilation (Battellini *et al.*, 2021). Paragraph 3 describes the main steps carried out to fill in the IF and presents the results and main achievements of the pilot exercise with reference to the supply and use tables, while the compilation of the environmental production account and environmental expenditure account is not dealt with in this chapter.

Finally, we draw some conclusions on the feasibility of compiling an integrated framework for countries that regularly produce monetary environmental accounts as well as on the implications in terms of policy use.

EUROSTAT'S LAYOUT FOR AN INTEGRATED MONETARY FRAMEWORK

Monetary environmental accounts also known as environmental activity accounts present monetary transactions carried out for the purpose of environmental protection and resource management.

The SEEA CF provides an accounting framework for representing four main kinds of monetary transactions. The first account concerns the expenditures of the general government, corporations, non-profit institutions, and households for the prevention and reduction of pollution (Environmental Protection Expenditure Account – EPEA). The second one reports the flow of the goods and services produced by the economy for environmental protection and for preserving resources from depletion (Environmental Goods and Services Sector account – EGSS). The third one relates to expenditures for resource management purposes following the same basic structure as outlined for the EPEA (Resource Management Expenditure Account – ReMEA). Finally, the fourth one accounts for the flows of environmental taxes and subsidies (Environmental subsidies and other transfers – ESST).

Within SEEA, each of the four monetary accounts has been designed for a specific purpose. The Integrated framework developed by Eurostat aims to provide a comprehensive picture of the actions and activities of economic operators for environmental purposes.

To this aim, the layout of the IF proposed by Eurostat includes a set of supply and use tables, and two flow accounts: production and expenditure.

This set of tables allows us to show balanced estimates on the:

- Supply, *i.e.*, which economic activity produces the environmental products (resources) available and for which environmental purpose based on the Classifications of Environmental Protection Activities (CEPA) and Resource Management Activities (CReMA) (Eurostat, 2020)?
- Use, *i.e.*, who uses the environmental products made available? for what kind of use (intermediate, final, investment, export)? and for which environmental purpose?
- Production, *i.e.*, the amount of value added generated by the production of environmental products, the amount of environmental output used as input for the production of environmental output (intermediate consumption of environmental products), the amount of output available for resident users;
- Expenditure, *i.e.*, how much the economy spends for an environmental purpose, including the investments in non-environmental products necessary for environmental purposes.

The remainder of this paragraph provides detailed explanations of the supply and use tables, whereas, as stated in the introduction, the environmental production account and environmental expenditure account are not dealt with in detail in this chapter.

Supply and use tables represent the macroeconomic equilibrium underlying national accounts, *i.e.*, all available resources produced on the economic territory of a country (detailed by economic activity) or imported from abroad (Supply Table) are used by the economy (Use Table): as intermediate inputs in the production process, as final consumption, as investments, as inventories or exported. In the national accounts, the representation is made according to a breakdown by groups of products according to the Classification of Products by Activity (CPA). In the integrated framework, the focus is limited to environmental goods and services, and the breakdown is based on environmental classification, CEPA, and CReMA.

The supply table of the integrated framework covers the following variables (see Fig. **1** for a simplified Supply Table):

	Output by ISIC industry				Imports	Taxes less subsidies on products	Trade and transport margins	Total supply
CEPA goods								
CEPA services								
CREMA goods								
CREMA services								

Fig. (1). Simplified supply table for environmental monetary accounts.

- Output at basic prices, by 6 International Standard Industry Classification (ISIC) categories;
- Imports;
- Taxes and subsidies on products;
- Trade and transport margins;
- Total supply at purchaser's prices (sum of the previous components).

Each variable is broken down by CEPA/CReMA and, within individual CEPA and CReMA, between goods and services (Fig. **1**). The breakdown of products into goods and services allows us to compare EPEA and EGSS estimates with respect to homogeneous categories (the final tables of the pilot Italian exercise apply a breakdown of products into 'cleaner' and 'specific').

Output includes market output, non-market output, ancillary activities, and output for own-final use.

The USE Table of the Integrated Framework covers the following variables (see Fig. **2** for a simplified Use Table):

	Intermediate consumption by ISC industry			Final consumption		Gross fixed capital formation			Exports	Total use
				General Gov.	Households	General Gov.	Specialized & secondary producers	Ancillary producers		
CEPA goods										
CEPA services										
CREMA goods										
CREMA services										

Fig. (2). Simplified use table for environmental monetary accounts.

- Intermediate consumption, by 6 ISIC categories;
- Final Consumption, By General Government (GG) and Households;
- Gross fixed capital formation;
- Exports;
- Total use at purchaser's prices (sum of the previous components).

Each variable is broken down by CEPA/CReMA and, for individual CEPAs and CReMAs, between goods and services (Fig. **2**).

How can the existing environmental monetary modules feed the integrated framework? Is the information covered by the SEEA monetary accounts sufficient to develop the tables proposed by Eurostat for the IF?

As already stated, EGSS has been specifically developed in order to present data on output and value added of environmental goods and services, representing a major source of information for the supply table and the production account.

On the other hand, EPEA has been designed mainly to calculate the National Expenditure on Environmental Protection (NEEP), which is typically a demand-side aggregate/indicator, thus covering the scope of both the use table and the expenditure account.

In principle, EGSS and EPEA could be used jointly to fulfill the tables of the IF, by using EGSS data for the supply table and the production account and EPEA for the use table and the expenditure account. The first step to assess to what extent EGSS and EPEA can be used in practice to compile IF Tables is the comparison of the scope of the two accounts in terms of coverage of products, activities, producers, and the kind of output. The comparison highlights that EPEA's and EGSS's scope, as defined by the Regulation on European Environmental Accounts (EEA) (EU, 2021b) were not fully homogeneous (Table **1**).

Table 1. Differences in scope between EGSS and EPEA.

SCOPE	EPEA	EGSS
Activities	Characteristic activities	Characteristic and non-characteristic activities
Products	Services	Goods and services
Environmental	Environmental Protection (EP)	Environmental Protection (EP) & Resource Management (RM)
Output	Market, non-market, and ancillary	Market
Producers	Market, non-market, and ancillary	Market

Source: Adapted from Table AN9-1: main features of EGSS and EPEA – EGSS Handbook, 2016 edition (Eurostat, 2016a).

The lack of a consistent scope for EPEA and EGSS implies that the compilation of a comprehensive integrated framework (*e.g.* encompassing both goods and services, all kinds of output and producers) cannot be simply derived from the combination of the two accounts.

Comparing the actual coverage of the two modules is the first step to assess which parts of the integrated framework can be fully compiled using the accounts as such, which parts need adjustments, and which parts need to be estimated. The subsequent steps are described below with reference to the Italian pilot application.

ITALIAN PILOT INTEGRATED FRAMEWORK

Italy, like other EU countries, regularly produces both EGSS and EPEA in compliance with the Regulation on Economic Environmental Accounts. The compilation of the IF Tables in the Italian pilot project was based on Italian EPEA and EGSS accounts with reference year 2016.

EGSS compulsory variables under the EU Regulation cover include: output, exports, gross value added, and employment corresponding to market activities, cross-classified by economic activities (NACE Rev. 2 A*21) and CEPA/CReMA classes.

EPEA compulsory variables under the EU Regulation cover Environmental Protection Services (EPS) only which include: output (market, non-market, and output of ancillary activities), intermediate consumption of EPS by corporations' specialist producers, imports and exports, Value Added Tax (VAT) and other taxes minus subsidies on products, gross fixed capital formation and acquisitions minus disposals of non-financial non-produced assets for the production of environmental protection services, final consumption of environmental protection services, and transfers (received/paid). Data are broken down by the institutional sector and the coverage in terms of CEPA categories varies according to the variable.

Supply and Use Tables of the IF – Main Compilation Steps

The regularly produced EGSS and EPEA allow us to compile only part of the variables and products of the IF Supply Table (Fig. **3**).

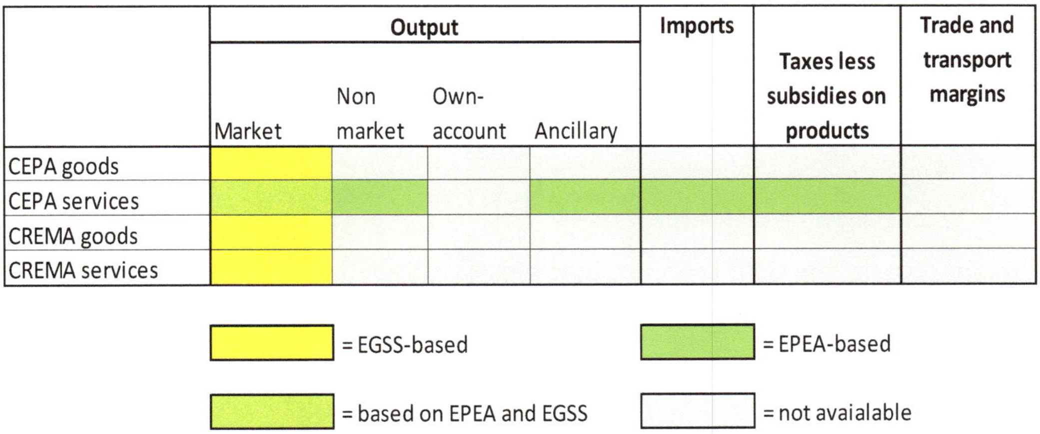

Fig. (3). Coverage of supply aggregates by italian EA.

The market output of environmental protection services is the only variable where a potential overlap exists between the two accounts that both report it.

For this reason, a specific comparison of EGSS and EPEA market output estimates was carried out (Table **2**).

Table 2. Comparison between market output estimates – EGSS and EPEA, italy, of the year 2016 (Billion Euros).

CEPA	-	MARKET OUTPUT	
		EGSS	EPEA
CEPA 1	Goods Services	1,423 535	-
CEPA 2	Goods Services	2,239 4,806	4,784
CEPA 3	Goods Services	460 23,736	21,680
CEPA 4	Goods Services	1,712 2,340	1,526

(Table 2) cont.....

CEPA	-	MARKET OUTPUT	
		EGSS	EPEA
CEPA 5	Goods Services	240 5	-
CEPA 6	Goods Services	25 17	0
CEPA 7	Goods Services	1 193	-
CEPA 8	Goods Services	0 32	0
CEPA 9	Goods Services	0 239	0
TOTAL CEPAs	Goods Services	6,109 31,902	0 27,990

The analysis of the data reported in the table allowed to highlight the following results with respect to services:

- For CEPA 2, 3, and 4, both EGSS and EPEA report data on the output of services produced by market producers, but EGSS estimates are higher. This is due to the larger coverage of services by EGSS. In addition to data on typical services of each CEPA, EGSS reports also provide estimates related to the following services: 'Architectural and engineering services for water, wastewater, waste management projects', 'Environmental consulting', 'Supporting services to organic agriculture', 'Maintenance, repair and installation services of environmental products';
- For CEPA 1, 5, 6, 7, 8, 9: EPEA market output estimates are not available.

The comparison of EGSS and EPEA estimates on output highlights that EGSS has higher coverage than EPEA as far as market output is concerned. For this reason, EGSS was selected as the primary source of market output for the preliminary compilation of the Supply Table.

As in the case of the supply table, prior to the actual compilation of the USE Table with EGSS and EPEA data for Italy, a preliminary evaluation was undertaken in order to:

- Identify potential overlapping between EPEA and EGSS;
- Assess the suitability of the available data for the IF table.

The only possible overlapping in the case of demand side variables with EGSS concerns EXPORTS, which are mandatory variables in both cases.

Under the EPEA framework, exports only concern services, whereas in EGSS, they cover both goods and services. EGSS provides a larger coverage, even though EGSS reports only on exports of products that are domestically produced.

As far as intermediate consumption and gross fixed capital formation are concerned, data reported under EPEA fulfill a different purpose with respect to the requirement of the integrated framework. In the latter, the demand aggregates (in particular intermediate consumption and gross fixed capital formation) refer to goods and services for environmental protection thus counterbalancing the same products on the supply side. By contrast, mandatory EPEA data include:

- Intermediate consumption of environmental protection products excludes goods and, with respect to services, it is limited only to some of them reported only for producers of environmental services;
- Gross fixed capital formation includes both environmental and, in some cases, non-environmental protection goods and, in case of non-environmental producers (ancillary producers), it is reported only for the manufacturing sector (specifically NACE 6-36).

Hence, the coverage of the IF Use Table by EGSS and EPEA data was very limited (Fig. **4**).

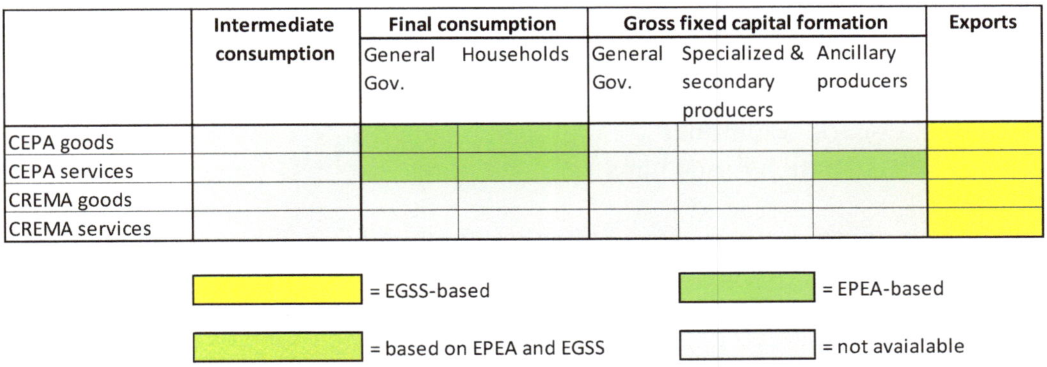

Fig. (4). Coverage of demand aggregates by italian EA.

The very first limitation highlighted by the exercise is the lack of estimates for resource management activities and products on the demand side. While EGSS covers resource management output, resource management is out of scope in EPEA and no estimation of ReMEA accounts is carried out in Italy.

For this reason, in the Italian pilot project, IF Tables were only compiled for the Environmental Protection (EP) domain and, specifically for CEPAs 1-4.

For the selected CEPAs, the use of EPEA and EGSS data directly allowed to compile part of the IF Tables, mainly by using EGSS for the supply side and EPEA for the demand side as shown in (Figs. **4** and **5**) above (non-market production is based on EPEA). However, as described in the previous paragraph, since the accounts have differences in scope and variables, the compilation of an integrated framework could not be simply derived from the combination of the two accounts.

With respect to CEPA categories, on the supply side, the existing data sources offer partial coverage for variables, such as imports, and taxes minus subsidies on products, trade, and transport margins. They are not covered by EGSS and, although EPEA covers them, its scope on the supply side only encompasses services, thus excluding environmental protection goods whose output is included in EGSS from the coverage of imports, taxes minus subsidies on products, trade, and transport margins (only a subset of products are currently covered by imports, trade and transport margins, while no estimates of 'trade and transport margins' are available in EPEA).

On the demand side, in many cases, EPEA data fulfill a different purpose than the IF.

Due to the very limited coverage of supply and demand aggregates by EPEA and EGSS, a number of additional steps were needed to estimate variables not available within EPEA/EGSS, namely:

- Identification of additional sources and methods, for example, coefficients derived from national accounts (*e.g.*, imports, exports, taxes less subsidies, margins);
- Balancing of supply and use equation (*e.g.* for uses of environmental goods);
- Final reduction of discrepancies.

The following paragraph presents the main results of the exercise.

Supply and Use Tables of the IF – Main Results

The additional steps carried out in addition to the direct EPEA and EGSS-based compilation allowed us to compile supply and use tables of the integrated framework for Italy for CEPAs 1-4 (Tables **3** and **4**). For each product included in EGSS estimates for CEPAs 1-4, the possible uses on the demand side (intermediate consumption, households' final consumption, General Government (GG) final consumption, Gross fixed capital formation (GFCF)) are identified (the products covered by the Italian pilot exercise are a subset of the products to be included in EGSS as for the Indicative Compendium - IC).

Table 3. Supply table for environmental protection in Italy, Year 2016 (Billions of Euros).

CEPA Classification	Output At Basic Prices						Total Output	Imports	Taxes Less Subsides On Products	Trade and Transport Margins	Total Supply Purchasers' Prices
	ISIC A	ISIC B	ISIC C	ISIC D-E	ISIC F	ISIC G-U	basic prices				
CEPA 1	**0**	**0**	**1,930**	**0**	**0**	**639**	**2,569**	**465**	**38**	**385**	**3,457**
Specific products	0	0	1904	0	0	639	2543	416	38	377	3374
Cleaner products	0	0	26	0	0	0	26	49	0	8	83
CEPA 2	**0**	**0**	**2,075**	**5,306**	**0**	**773**	**8,154**	**327**	**255**	**296**	**9,032**
Specific products	0	0	2075	5306	0	773	8154	327	255	296	9032
Cleaner products	0	0	0	0	0	0	0	0	0	0	0
CEPA 3	**0**	**7**	**3,285**	**14,638**	**0**	**10,392**	**28,322**	**320**	**1,698**	**316**	**30,656**
Specific products	0	7	3285	14638	0	10392	28322	320	1698	316	30656
Cleaner products	0	0	0	0	0	0	0	0	0	0	0
CEPA 4	**1,096**	**0**	**178**	**1,584**	**7**	**74**	**2,939**	**462**	**83**	**637**	**4,121**
Specific products	89	0	178	1584	7	74	1932	30	59	18	2039
Cleaner products	1007	0	0	0	0	0	1007	432	24	619	2082
Other CEPAs	**n.a.**	**n.a.**	**n.a.**	**n.a.**	**n.a.**	**n.a.**	**n.a.**	**n.a.**	**n.a.**	**n.a.**	**n.a.**
Specific products	n.a.	n.a.	n.a.	n.a.	n.a.	n.a.	n.a.	n.a.	n.a.	n.a.	n.a.
Cleaner products	n.a.	n.a.	n.a.	n.a.	n.a.	n.a.	n.a.	n.a.	n.a.	n.a.	n.a.
Total EP	**1,096**	**7**	**7,468**	**21,528**	**7**	**11,878**	**41,984**	**1,574**	**2,074**	**1,634**	**47,266**

Table 4. Use table for environmental protection in Italy, Year 2016 (Billions of Euros).

CEPA Classification	Intermediate Consumption						Total Intermediate Consumption	Final consumption		Gross Fixed Capital Formation	Exports	Total Use At Purchasers' Prices
	ISIC A	ISIC B	ISIC C	ISIC D-E	ISIC F	ISIC G-U		general Government	Households			
CEPA 1	**14**	**1**	**637**	**41**	**323**	**413**	**1,429**	**441**	**63**	**581**	**943**	**3,457**
Specific products	14	1	637	41	323	413	1,429	441	50	524	930	3,374
Cleaner products	0	0	0	0	0	0	0	0	13	57	13	83

(Table 4) cont.....

CEPA Classification	Intermediate Consumption						Total Intermediate Consumption	Final consumption		Gross Fixed Capital Formation	Exports	Total Use At Purchasers' Prices
	ISIC A	ISIC B	ISIC C	ISIC D-E	ISIC F	ISIC G-U		general Government	Households			
CEPA 2	**261**	**33**	**1,125**	**1,065**	**404**	**1,292**	**4,180**	**404**	**2,409**	**1,008**	**1,031**	**9,032**
Specific products	261	33	1125	1065	404	1292	4,180	404	2,409	1,008	1,031	9,032
Cleaner products	0	0	0	0	0	0	0	0	0	0	0	0
CEPA 3	**117**	**75**	**3,041**	**3,183**	**2,489**	**12,877**	**21,782**	**955**	**6,964**	**618**	**337**	**30,656**
Specific products	117	75	3041	3183	2489	12877	21,782	955	6,964	618	337	30,656
Cleaner products	0	0	0	0	0	0	0	0	0	0	0	0
CEPA 4	**91**	**52**	**979**	**595**	**138**	**664**	**2,519**	**12**	**1,238**	**133**	**219**	**4,121**
Specific products	46	52	521	595	138	553	1,905	12	0	120	2	2,039
Cleaner products	45	0	458	0	0	111	614	0	1,238	13	217	2,082
Other CEPAs	**n.a.**	**n.a.**	**n.a.**	**n.a.**	**n.a.**	**n.a.**	**n.a.**	**n.a.**	**n.a.**	**n.a.**	**n.a.**	**n.a.**
Specific products	n.a.	n.a.	n.a.	n.a.	n.a.	n.a.	n.a.	n.a.	n.a.	n.a.	n.a.	n.a.
Cleaner products	n.a.	n.a.	n.a.	n.a.	n.a.	n.a.	n.a.	n.a.	n.a.	n.a.	n.a.	n.a.
Total EP	**483**	**161**	**5,782**	**4,884**	**3,354**	**15,246**	**29,910**	**1,812**	**10,674**	**2,340**	**2,530**	**47,266**

Among the improvements achieved through the estimated supply and use tables, three are the main ones.

The first one relates to the enhanced analytical robustness of balanced estimates compared to stand-alone numbers. In the case of Italy, environmental monetary accounts estimates are consistent with balanced national accounts data and this ensures that no major discrepancies occur between supply and demand. Nonetheless, balancing the environmental accounts data for the purposes of the IF allowed us to improve their consistency.

The second relates to the enhanced analytical potential of the supply and use framework, with respect to the partial perspective adopted by the traditional (not integrated) accounting frameworks.

Finally, from a quantitative standpoint, integration brought about an increase in the coverage of the estimates. With regard to the output of environmental protection for CEPAs 1-4, the estimated 42 billion of total output at basic prices (Table **2**), is significantly higher than the corresponding estimate for EGSS (37 billion euros) and EPEA (around 28 billion euros) for the same CEPAs available prior to the pilot exercise (Table **1**).

The difference between the IF output estimate and the EGSS one (almost 5 billion euros) is mainly explained by the increased coverage of products (IF estimates cover 'Electric and more resource efficient transport equipment' not previously available) as well as by the expansion of the scope beyond market output to encompass non-market output, ancillary output, and output for the own final use (for organic agriculture).

The difference between the IF output estimate and the EPEA one (almost 15 billion euros) is mainly explained by the increased coverage of services (IF estimates cover 'Architectural and engineering services for water, wastewater, waste management projects', 'Environmental consulting', 'Supporting services to organic agriculture', 'Maintenance, repair, and installation services of environmental products', also covered by the Italian EGSS and not by the Italian EPEA) and the inclusion of goods (not covered in the EPEA output).

Furthermore, the estimated 47 billion of total supply at purchaser's prices was obtained by estimating imports, taxes less subsidies on products, trade, and transport margins for all environmental products included, thus significantly enlarging the coverage of EPEA for the same variables.

CONCLUSION

The pilot implementation carried out for Italy allowed us to check, for the first time, the consistency of environmental accounts and monetary aggregates within a Supply and Use accounting framework as well as within a complete production and expenditure account.

Due to the lack of estimates for resource management activities and products on the demand side, CEPA categories could only be covered in the pilot project. With respect to CEPA categories, on the supply side, the existing data sources offer partial coverage for variables, such as imports, and taxes minus subsidies on products, trade, and transport margins. They are not covered by EGSS and, although EPEA covers them, its scope on the supply side only encompasses services, thus excluding EP goods whose output is included in EGSS from the coverage of imports, taxes minus subsidies on products, trade and transport margins.

On the demand side, EPEA obligatory variables under the EU Economic Environmental Accounts Regulation are often not in line with the purpose of the integrated framework.

The main additional problems in using EPEA as a data source relate to the difference in scope between EPEA and the Use Table.

Due to the differences listed above, data sources additional to EPEA and EGSS are needed to estimate part of the demand aggregate responding to IF requirements.

The work carried out to estimate missing items and fill in the gaps identified in the preliminary compilation process shows that it is possible to significantly enlarge the coverage in terms of products of EPEA and EGSS reporting.

The exercise carried out in Italy is an example of how, by combining existing environmental accounts, new sources, and national accounts balancing techniques, the available information on transactions for environmental purposes can be greatly enhanced. This effort goes in the direction of introducing innovations in official statistics to meet the increasing EU policy information requirements, such as those related to the European Green Deal and the integration of sustainability-related criteria into European policies. However, the scope of the Italian pilot exercise needs to be enlarged to encompass high-priority areas such as, *e.g.*, energy efficiency and energy from renewable sources, in order to provide comprehensive climate, energy, and environmental transition-related statistical information.

CHAPTER 7

Modernization of the Economic Accounts for Agriculture in the EU

Cecilia Pop[1,*] and **Angela Piersante**[1]

[1] *Eurostat, Luxembourg, Luxembourg*

Abstract: This chapter presents issues related to the modernisation of the economic accounts for agriculture since 2017 (Eurostat, 2022). The methodological aspects and the transmission deadlines of the Economic Accounts for Agriculture (EAA) are set up in Regulation (EC) No 138/2004 Annex I (EU, 2004) and follow closely the SNA 2008 (UNSTAT, 2009) and the ESA 2010 (Eurostat, 2013).

Eurostat's effort in the modernization of EAA is an example of the direction to follow and the potential of these satellite accounts for the core system of national accounts in SNA.

Keywords: Common agricultural policy, Economic accounts for agriculture, Indicators, Modernization process, Sustainable development goals, Total factor productivity.

INTRODUCTION

European Union (EU) policies require, for their implementation and adaptation over time, comparable and reliable statistical information from the member states on all the different components of sustainability: economic, social, territorial and environmental. Eurostat's official statistics enable the various policy actors to assess the current state of the Union and to adopt the most appropriate measures for future development.

Specifically, European agricultural statistics provide data for the Common Agricultural Policy (CAP) and fisheries, as well as information on the environment, food safety and farm animal health. The 'Strategy for Agricultural Statistics for 2020 and beyond' is the major programme in the Union to modernise these statistics run by the European Commission jointly with Member States (Eurostat, 2015b).

* **Corresponding author Cecilia Pop:** Eurostat, Luxembourg, Luxembourg; E-mail: cecilia.pop@ec.europa.eu

This strategy includes the following key objectives:

- Produce high quality statistics that meet users' needs efficiently and effectively;
- Improve the harmonisation and coherence of European agricultural statistics.

These are the objectives of the European Statistical System Committee (ESSC) and are reflected in the Regulatory Fitness and Performance (REFIT) program that would like to improve the overall European System of Agricultural Statistics (EASS). International recommendations on reporting greenhouse gas emissions by the Intergovernmental Panel on Climate Change (IPCC) and the standards provided by the UN Food and Agriculture Organization (FAO) are included in the European strategy. This is also in line with the UN Global Strategy to improve agricultural and rural statistics.

Finally, agriculture is at the core of the European Green Deal, specifically for the 'Farm-to-Fork strategy' (EC, 2020).

The European Commission, EU Council and Parliament need this relevant information as a substantial share of the EU budget is allocated to the CAP (Eurostat, 2022), which is nearly 40% of the Union's total budget in the context of the 2014-2020 Multiannual Financial Framework (MFF).

As said, a priority of the European Commission is to have modernized statistics for the European Green Deal, within the Farm-to-Fork and Biodiversity strategies.

Agricultural accounts considered here are at the core of the agricultural statistics system and provide information for sustainable development. With this approach, social objectives and rural development policy are together with competitiveness and economic sustainability of production. Furthermore, these accounts are increasingly needed to understand the effects of climate change and regional policies that impact local development.

This instrument allows us to meet the main quality criteria for statistical data: to be consistent and comparable. The Union legislation provides the common statistical standards, concepts and reporting formats.

In summary, today we can observe that Eurostat has compiled a full set of European agricultural statistics and accounts for decades, covering several aspects: structure of farms, economic performances (including labour input), animal and crop production, organic farming, agricultural prices, pesticides, nutrients and other agri-environmental aspects. All of them are important to support the EU policy decision-making for sustainable development.

The Economic Accounts for Agriculture

The performance of the agricultural sector in the EU, as a whole, can be assessed with the volume and price changes for agricultural goods and services in the frame of an accounts system. The Economic Accounts for Agriculture (EAA) provide macroeconomic-level information about the agricultural output and inputs (costs, investment, land and labour) to key users.

Annual macroeconomic information is provided to European policymakers with the first estimates in November (before the end of the same year), the second in January the year after, followed by (semi)final data in September.

EAA follow the methodology for national accounts as a satellite account of the European System of Accounts (ESA 2010). However, their compilation requires specific rules and methods, set out by Regulation (EC) No 138/2004 and later amendments of the European Parliament and of the Council (EU, 2004).

National and regional economic accounts for agriculture have been produced and transmitted to Eurostat by Member states since 2000. An assessment in 2016 by Eurostat found that an update was necessary to consider changes in the sector and EU policy priorities.

The Modernisation Process Started Already in 2017

The updating of European agricultural statistics, including the EAA, is carried out by Eurostat within the European Statistical System (ESS), building on a long-standing partnership with the National Statistical Institutes (NSIs) and the other concerned authorities.

As indicated in the 'Strategy for Agricultural Statistics for 2020 and Beyond', "the main categories of stakeholders of European agricultural statistics are data producers (NSIs and other national authorities as well as Eurostat), respondents (farmers, farmers' organisations and businesses) and users (public and private decision-makers - in particular other Commission departments - researchers and journalists). They have been consulted extensively on problems and desired changes in the status quo, their data needs and priorities, possible policy options to solve the problems, impacts of suggested actions, and the formulation of the strategy" (EU, 2022b).

The evaluation of this strategy included in the Special Report SR 01/2016 by the European Court of Auditors audit provides some indications of the extent to which EAA satisfy the data needs of the users (ECA, 2016). These results are also important drivers for the modernisation of the EAA.

Since the beginning of 2018, Eurostat, assisted by the Working Group on "Agricultural Accounts and Prices" (AAP WG) and the Directors' Group for "Agricultural Statistics" (DGAS) established and pursued a number of priorities in the context of modernisation of EAA.

Modernisation of EAA in Eurostat is a two-fold purpose process: on one hand, to work on updating the EAA methodology to take into account the ESA provisions and the evolution of the agricultural sector and, on the other hand, to automate, as much as possible the production, validation and dissemination of the data.

One of the priorities was to align the EAA regulation (EC) No 138/2004 of the European Parliament and of the Council to the ESA 2010 provisions. This was achieved with the adoption of Commission Regulation 2018/280 (EU, 2018).

At the same time, Eurostat performed a study to examine whether the EAA can be further developed to provide a reasonable estimate of the economic value of public goods produced by farmers.

Finally, with a view of providing good quality and comparable EAA data, including the Agricultural Labour Input (ALI), to users and, especially, to the Directorate General Agriculture and Rural Development (DG AGRI), the definition of Annual Work Units (AWU) in agriculture was analysed in depth. The purpose was to ascertain if the use of farmers' incomes per AWU in absolute terms was a meaningful indicator. It was concluded that it can be difficult to compare farmers' income across countries, especially when the input profile of capital and labour in agriculture is very different.

EU Sustainable Development Goals – Zero Hunger

The CAP has among its objectives to ensure a fair standard of living for farmers, improving agricultural productivity and the incomes of food producers. These are key factors in achieving one of the EU Sustainable Development Goals (SDGs): "towards ending hunger and malnutrition" (Eurostat, 2017-2022).

One of the indicators used to monitor progress towards ensuring access to safe, nutritious and sufficient food is 'agricultural factor income per annual work unit'. This indicator is expressed in SDGs as an index (so-called 'Indicator A', explained below) and in absolute values, based on the EAA data (Eurostat, 2001a).

However, as mentioned above, statisticians find it difficult to compare the net factor income between countries that have high capital input and low labour input in this sector with countries that show opposite inputs. One explanation is that the number of working hours per AWU can differ among the countries, affecting the comparison of the absolute levels of agricultural factor income per AWU. Furthermore, it can be difficult to measure the inputs related to small farms.

Agricultural Labour Productivity – The 'Indicator A'

Indicator A is an index that measures the real income of factors in agriculture per annual work units (AWU) and corresponds to the index of the real net value added at factor cost (called 'factor income') of agriculture per total AWUs.

It provides a yardstick to compare the economic performance of the agricultural industry over time between Member States and as a whole for EU aggregates, in relation to a base year.

It should not be confused with the total income of farming households or the income of a person working in agriculture.

Indicator A growth can be defined as the ratio between the change in factor incomes in real terms (adjusted for inflation) over a considered period and the corresponding change in labour input used to produce value-added and hence measures the growth in productivity over a given time span. An increase in Indicator A reflects a gain in value-added, which is not generated by an increase in labour input, yet it reveals the joint effects of many factors including new technologies, as well as changes in the organization of production.

As an example, the figure below provides a snapshot of efficiency in the agricultural industry by reporting the trends of indicator A and its key components at the level of EU-27 (2010=100) (Fig. **1**):

It shows that since 2017, there has been a levelling off of agricultural income per AWU for the EU as a whole, after a fluctuation lasting several years after 2005. This has reflected a recent decline in factor income, accompanied by a continuous contraction in labour input. However, agricultural income per AWU for the EU as a whole in 2020 was estimated to be 27.2% higher than the 2010 level.

Data Sets and Formulas

Within the EAA data domain, the data sets used to calculate Indicator A are provided by each country, three times per year, and relate to:

- Value of factor income at current prices in national currency (NAC), which is the gross value added adjusted for the consumption of fixed capital, subsidies and taxes on production;

- Agricultural labour input, expressed by AWUs, which defines the volume of work done in full-time work equivalents and includes part-time, seasonal and unsalaried labour input in agriculture.

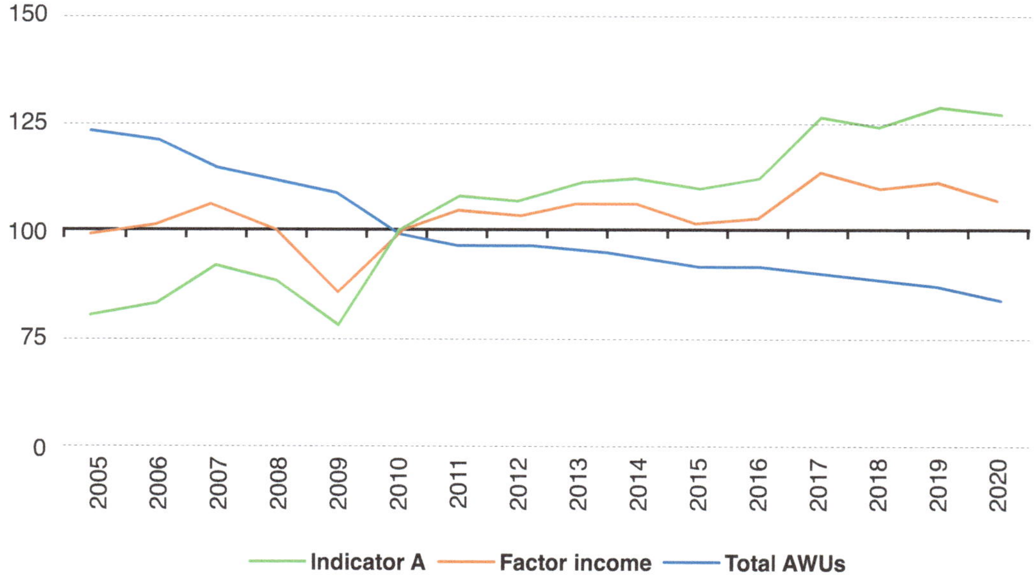

Fig. (1). Trend in indicator A and components in EU-27 (2010=100). Source: Eurostat (Statistics explained: Performance of the agricultural sector, 2021).

Moreover, in line with the EU methodology in Annex I of Regulation 138/2004 (EU, 2004), the GDP implicit price index (the GDP deflator) at the country level is the deflator used to compute the real values and indices of EAA data as well as the exchange rates, provided by Eurobase, are applied to calculate the country data in euro.

Below are reported the formulas (using the base year 2010, as an example) to compute Indicator A for:

- **Each country**

$$\textit{Real Value Index}_t^{2010} = \frac{(\textit{Factor income Value}_t^n \textit{NAC} / \textit{Exch.rate}_{2010}^{2010} / \textit{GDP}_t^{2010} * 100)}{(\textit{Factor income Value}_{2010}^{2010} / \textit{Exch.rate}_{2010}^{2010})} * 100$$

$$\textit{Total AWU Index}_t^{2010} = \frac{\textit{Total AWU}_t^n}{\textit{Total AWU}_{2010}^{2010}} * 100$$

$$\textit{Indicator } A_t^{2010} = \frac{\textit{Real Value Index}_t^{2010}}{\textit{Total AWU Index}_t^{2010}} * 100$$

Where:

n = the year referring to the prices

t = the year referring to the data

- **EU aggregate**

$$EU27\ Real\ Value\ Index_t^{2010} = \frac{\left(\sum_{27}^{C=1} Factor\ income\ Value_{t,c}^{n}\ NAC / Exch.rate_{2010,c}^{2010} / GDP_{t,c}^{2010} * 100\right)}{\left(\sum_{27}^{C=1} Factor\ income\ Value_{2010,c}^{2010} / Exch.rate_{2010,c}^{2010}\right)} * 100$$

$$EU27\ Total\ AWU\ Index_t^{2010} = \frac{\sum_{27}^{C=1} Total\ AWU_{t,c}^{n}}{\sum_{27}^{C=1} Total\ AWU_{2010,c}^{2010}} * 100$$

$$EU27\ Indicator\ A_t^{2010} = \frac{EU27\ Real\ Value\ Index_t^{2010}}{EU27\ Total\ AWU\ Index_t^{2010}} * 100$$

Where:

n = the year referring to the prices

t = the year referring to the data

let c =1 to 27 referring to country data of EU27 aggregate 8

AGRICULTURAL TOTAL FACTOR PRODUCTIVITY

"Productivity isn't everything, but in the long run, it is almost everything. A country's ability to improve its standard of living over time depends almost entirely on its ability to raise its output per worker" (Krugman, 1994).

The European Commission in the "Annual Sustainable Growth Strategy 2020 identified productivity gains as one of the four dimensions of EU economic policy enabling to guide structural reforms, investment and responsible fiscal policies in the years to come" (EC, 2019).

In line with the Growth Strategy 2020, Eurostat is carrying out initiatives to develop productivity measures within national accounts. With regard to the agriculture sector, the agricultural total factor productivity (TFP) growth gives a measure of productivity growth that reflects improvements in the efficiency with which farmers combine inputs (labour, capital and land) to produce outputs. Monitoring the progress made using this index helps to obtain a first analysis of the production growth evolution, at the same time allowing evaluation of the saving of resources and the improvement of the sustainability of an economic system.

For this purpose, Eurostat joined the OECD Network on Agricultural Total Factor Productivity and the Environment, whose aim is to develop a framework for cross-country agricultural TFP comparisons. Since 2017, when it was established, the OECD Network has already held several meetings, mainly discussing TFP with regard to methodological issues, policies and data collection (OECD, 2022).

In due course, the objective is to create a set of "environmentally-adjusted" TFP (EATFP) indicators, and develop methodological and practical guidance specific to TFP and EATFP measurement in agriculture in the form of a manual, based on the current OECD "Measuring Productivity" (OECD, 2001). The manual, still in progress, will be an important resource for countries to use when building a production account for agriculture and will serve in achieving consistency in methods and data among countries.

For the time being, Eurostat is still collecting and providing data only on labour productivity, Indicator A. This indicator does not use a quality-adjusted labour input, as is the case for the EU Quality Adjusted Labour Input compiled by national accounts (Eurostat, 2016b). However, it can be described as "...a useful measure: it relates to the single most important factor of production, is intuitively appealing and relatively easy to measure. Also, labour productivity is a key determinant of living standards, measured as per capita income, and from this perspective, it is of significant relevance. However, it only partially reflects the productivity of labour in terms of the personal capacities of workers or the intensity of their efforts. Labour productivity reflects how efficiently labour is combined with other factors of production, how many of these other inputs are available per worker and how rapidly embodied and disembodied technical change proceeds. This makes labour productivity a good starting point for the analysis of some of these factors. One way of carrying out further analysis is to turn to multifactor productivity (MFP) measures" (OECD, 2001).

Although Indicator A is useful synthetic information to analyse the evolution of the performance agricultural industry for each Member State and at the level of the EU, in a future perspective of modernisation of EAA, it would be desirable to produce more complete productivity measures in agriculture.

CONCLUSION

Among the main recommendations of the above-mentioned ECA Special Report was to ensure the transmission of regional-level data based on formal arrangements with the Member States and quality reporting for EAA. Eurostat has collected these data since the beginning of 2000 from almost all Member States.

From the EU legal perspective, in February 2021, the European Commission adopted the proposal of an amending act to Regulation (EC) 138/2004 to formalise this reporting. The amending regulation was discussed with the European Parliament and the Council.

At the same time, Eurostat, assisted by Member States experts, is working on ascertaining if the agricultural accounts could be further developed to use their full potential to provide information on other factors impacting farmers' income. Specifically, to the sector, improvements could be on: the role of imports, developments in demand for agricultural products (domestic or foreign), supply to the food industry, final consumption by households, special treatment of agriculture in the tax system or the use for non-food purpose such as the production of bioenergy. All these are important factors that could impact farmers' incomes.

Extensions of EAA are technically possible if required by policymakers, to take account of overall sustainability: environmental and social issues of this sector of activity.

DISCLAIMER

This chapter is based on a paper presented by the authors in the "International Conference on Accounting & Assessment in Statistics (ICAAS)", Luxembourg, 31 May – 4 June 2021.

CHAPTER 8

Public Sector and Government Accounts

Edoardo Pizzoli[1,*]

[1] *Department of Finance, University of Luxembourg, Luxembourg, Luxembourg*

Abstract: The specific sub-system of national accounts dedicated to the public sector deserves careful analysis since through this, the main public policy actions can be monitored by statisticians. With great care, in the System of National Accounts (SNA) and the European System of Accounts (ESA) in the EU, public sector and government accounts are brought into the framework and firmly linked within the core system of national accounts. This is a required coherence effort as there is a long history of public sector accounts and, normally, a double accounting with different criteria is carried out by the public institutions in European countries. The basic frame and definitions will be introduced in this chapter, underlining the problems but also the necessity of this great effort at the accounting level.

This challenge represents a frontier for accounting research for the purposes of monitoring policies for sustainable development.

Keywords: Functional classification, Government finance, Government accounts, Public sector accounting, Sustainable development policies.

INTRODUCTION

In this chapter, we present the specific system of accounts developed for the main actor in the economy: the so-called 'government' or, more extensively, the 'public administration' operating in each country at several territorial levels. A specific sector of units (the 'Public Sector') and accounts (the 'Government Accounts' and 'Public Sector Accounts') is defined in the UN System of National Accounts (SNA) manual and the EU version of the European System of Accounts (ESA) (UNSTAT, 2009; Eurostat, 2013).

"The flexibility of the SNA is further illustrated with the public sector, whose components are systematically shown at various levels of detail in the classification of institutional sectors. The components of the public sector may be rearranged to group the accounts of the overall public sector. These accounts may

* **Corresponding author Edoardo Pizzoli:** Department of Finance, University of Luxembourg, Luxembourg, Luxembourg; E-mail: edoardo.pizzoli@uni.lu

be shown before consolidation and after consolidation to describe the relations between the public sector and the private sector and between the public sector and the rest of the world (by separating the external transactions of the public sector)" (SNA, par. 2.162).

SNA provides the "international standards for ... public accounting" (SNA, Preface, B, xlvii). The manual defines the macro-economic accounting principles in response to developments in accounting standards for government, public corporations, and public-private partnerships. How to record transactions between units within the sector and with units in other sectors of the economy.

The ESA Manual follows the SNA standards, providing further definitions and classifications for specific cases.

PUBLIC SECTOR ACCOUNTS

"The public sector consists of general government and public corporations" (ESA, par. 20.303).

Resident institutional units operating in the economy are included in this specific sector based on the "government control principle" (SNA, par. 4.26; ESA, par. 20.309). Specific attention is devoted to this key classification feature of public units and to borderline cases in SNA and ESA manuals (SNA, par. 4.23 and 4.77; ESA, par. 20.309).

"The elements composing the public sector are already present in the main sector structure of the system and can be rearranged to compile the public sector accounts. This is undertaken by putting together the subsectors of the general government sector and the public subsectors of non-financial and financial corporations" (ESA, par. 20.303).

"Public sector accounts may be constructed according to the ESA framework and sequence of accounts, and in principle, both consolidated and unconsolidated versions are analytically useful. Alternative presentations, such as the ... Government Finance Statistics presentation ... are also useful" (ESA, par. 20.305).

Government Accounts

This system of accounts covers the 'general government' broken down into its hierarchical and territorially defined sub-sectors: Central Government, State Government (for Federal political organizations), Local Government, and Social Security Funds (SNA, par. 4.129; ESA, par. 2.113). The accounts of each sub-sector may be presented independently.

Specific accounts are also compiled for some units belonging to this sector: non-market institutions such as agencies, institutes, and non-profit institutions (NPIs) controlled by the government.

Public Corporations Accounts

Public corporations are controlled by the government and follow the same accounting rules as private corporations.

"One common sub-sectoring (of the institutional sectors) is to identify those non-financial and financial corporations that are controlled by the government, called public corporations" (SNA, par. 4.34).

Their peculiarities can be related to the sectors of activity in which they operate, considered strategic or necessary to require public support at the central or territorial level of the government. Public corporations are created or acquired "when a government unit wishes to intervene in the sphere of production" (SNA, par. 4.120).

The Development of Public Accounts

Public accounts are organised according to the hierarchical organisation of the institutional units within the public sector, as follows (Fig. **1**):

Each subsystem of accounts, corresponding to the previous regroupings of units, has a different territorial reference and economic size.

The transition from accounts of a lower hierarchical level to those of a higher level requires an aggregation, called 'consolidation', which requires the clearing of transactions that occur between units within the system represented by the level in question.

Complexity and Consistency Issues

This system of accounts is particularly complex given the size of the public sector and the number of units operating in this sector of the economy. In addition, some specific transactions are subject to special accounting rules that differ from the rest of the economy. Therefore, the overall system of public accounts is particularly problematic, with regard to some specific quality standards that require special attention from public authorities.

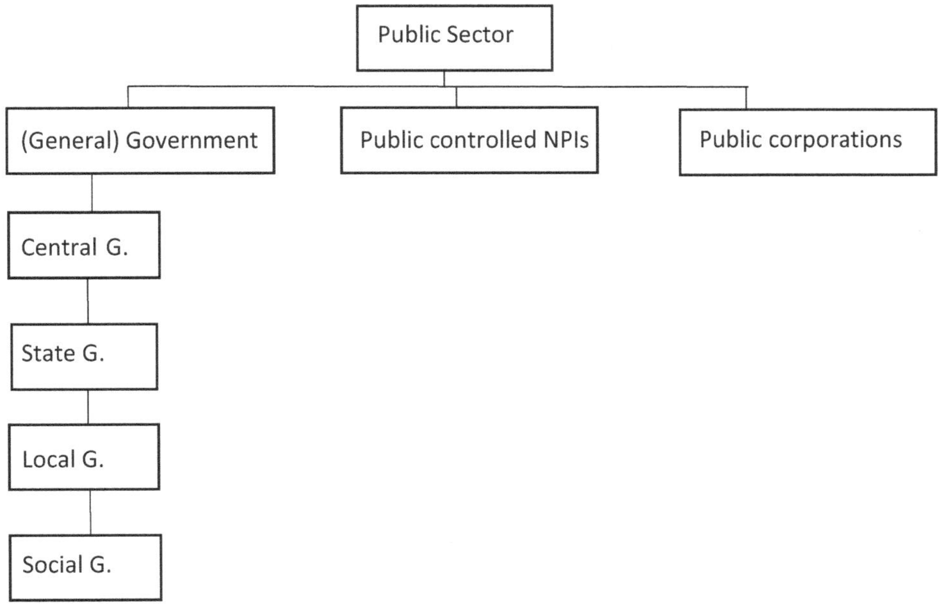

Fig. (1). Public sector organization and accounts.

For example, the methods of valuation of specific economic transactions and their recording, the consistency of transactions, and aggregation within each account and between related accounts must be ensured.

In addition, it can be a source of possible ambiguity and duplication of data that several public authorities usually keep stand-alone and independent sub-systems of accounts with different timing and data sources. All this can lead to possible sources of inconsistency for the same accounting items that require reconciliation of methods and values, through periodic revisions.

Government Finance and Debt

A key challenge for countries' economic policy is the financial stability of the Public Sector and, as a consequence, of the whole economy. The related accounts are fundamental to monitoring deficit and debt, through recording taxation and public expenditure: all items that determine the long-run path of the economy and its sustainability.

In Europe, for example, Eurostat maintains a system of public sector accounts that allows to produce Government Finance Statistics (GFS), showing the economic activities of governments, and the key indicators for the Excessive Deficit Procedure (EDP) analysis. This quarterly data covers the euro area, the EU and its Member States, also EFTA countries, and EU candidate countries.

Similar systems of accounts are available in different areas of the world and at the UN level to monitor the increasing global public debt (UN, 2023).

COFOG Classification for Sustainable Analysis

At the international level, a specific classification is available for public statistics and accounts, which makes it possible to classify public expenditure into two levels and thus to understand the resources allocated to different policy objectives. This is the Classification of the Functions of Government (COFOG), developed at the international level and with first-level data currently available for 33 of the 37 OECD countries (UN, 1980, 1993, 2000; Eurostat, 2019b; OECD, 2021).

Until recently, second-level COFOG data were available in some national statistical offices but were not collected by international organizations. Moreover, the second-level COFOG data were not always fully comparable among countries because the SNA/UN guide and the IMF Manual on Government Finance Statistics did not provide much practical information on the application of COFOG concepts.

This classification allows for the analysis of sustainability goals and related policies implemented by governments, which will be further developed within this classification.

CONCLUSION

The system of accounts developed for the public sector, given the economic relevance of the institutional units classified in this sector, is extremely important to study and develop specifically for monitoring sustainable development policies.

As has been acknowledged, the specificity of the public sector makes this system particularly articulated and in practice affected by difficulties of homogeneity, resulting in possible inconsistencies and the need for periodic revision processes over time.

For this reason, specific academic disciplines (public finance, financial science, public accounting, *etc.*) have been devoted to the study of this system and different schools of thought have developed in different countries. In national and international statistical institutions, specific offices keep and manage this system of accounts. Finally, technology also plays a crucial role in the development and improvement of the system.

The system's ability to provide quality information to support public policy decision-makers ultimately has a major impact on the economy and the expected future development processes towards long-term sustainability. In this respect, the evolution and improvement of this system are very important in order to maintain the time series of data consistent, but also to constantly introduce new information needed for this specific purpose.

PART III: Economic Sustainability Issues for Policy Makers: National Accounts Applications

CHAPTER 9

Output and GDP in National Accounts: Possible Dis-Aggregations and Reclassifications to Estimate Un-Observed and Neglected Areas of the Economy Relevant for Sustainability

Edoardo Pizzoli[1,*]

[1] *Department of Finance, University of Luxembourg, Luxembourg, Luxembourg*

Abstract: The definitions of output and Gross Domestic Product (GDP) are, in line with the UN System of National Accounts (SNA), intended to measure the total "human economic activity" over a territory and estimates have been developed by official statistical offices to calculate the economic aggregates.

A theoretical reclassification of their components would allow us to account for different categories of products and new types of producers. This is a useful exercise that can become a tool for supporting data collection and measuring the difficult components of these key national accounts aggregates. In addition, new subsystems of accounts, such as the UN Economic and Environmental Accounts (SEEA), can be developed from them, in support of core national estimates. They can provide data to calculate indicators on important environmental policies and to monitor the sustainability of development. From this point of view, studies on European countries such as Italy could provide instructive starting points for further research.

Keywords: Economic sustainability, GDP, National accounts, Output, Satellite accounting, Un-observed economy.

INTRODUCTION

Gross Domestic Product (GDP) is still a main indicator in the national account system even if now numerous authors from different authoritative parts consider it necessary to integrate and eventually overcome it (Costanza *et al.*, 2014). Yet, back to the national accounts developments after the Great Depression, during the 1930s, and later, after the Second World War, promoting GDP growth has remained the primary national policy goal in almost every country.

[*] **Corresponding author Edoardo Pizzoli:** Department of Finance, University of Luxembourg, Luxembourg, Luxembourg; E-mail: edoardo.pizzoli@uni.lu

Now, if we reconsider the rich information content behind this indicator, and specifically the main aggregate of Output, it is possible to estimate new sub-aggregates and calculate indicators that can be useful for a correct analysis of the development sustainability. Several extensions of the core national accounts system are actually proposed by the UN Statistics Division and by Eurostat integrating this important information system.

Output and GDP in ESA and SNA

The two base indicators for national accounting (Output and GDP) have been detailed and defined in the UN System of National Accounts (SNA) and accordingly by the EU European System of Accounts (ESA) in several editions of the national accounts' manuals (UNSTAT, 2009; Eurostat, 2013).

The main components of these aggregates are observable and measured by almost all the UN countries. Some of them are difficult to observe and collect the data or they are even not directly observable. There is an area of non-observed economy that includes underground economy, informal and illegal production that for economic and statistical reasons is missing in official Output and GDP and only in some cases estimated.

Furthermore, there is much-hidden information that is 'nested' within the aggregates, which is very useful for understanding development and its long-term sustainability.

Definition of Output in ESA

Based on the ESA definition "Output is the total of products created during the accounting period" (Eurostat, 2013; ESA, par. 3.14). Output is the aggregation of goods and services, *via* monetary prices, which are the result of a production process with a human involvement or direction (human production).

Behind the concept of output is, therefore, the concept of production: "an activity carried out under the control, responsibility, and management of an Institutional Unit (IU) that uses inputs of labour, capital and goods and services to produce outputs of goods and services" (ESA, par. 3.07).

"The ESA records all outputs that result from production within the production boundary" (ESA, par. 1.31). To set the boundary of an economy and make operational the inclusion/exclusion mechanism for statistical measurement, it requires a certain degree of approximation, that is the introduction of a degree of statistical error and the adoption of some conventions that guarantee the comparability of aggregates internally in the measurement system (*i.e.* EU comparability for ESA).

Based on this definition of the aggregate, that is why the production of goods and services as a natural process is excluded; such as, for example, the unmanaged growth of fish stocks in international waters (ESA, par. 3.07). The products are offered for free by nature so they are outside the economic boundary. Note that, this exclusion from economic output does not mean that the produced goods and services are not useful or needed for final or intermediate use (consumption or investment). If there is a human effort for management and 'extraction' of the natural resources, that is human work of employees, then this production enters into the economic boundary, and goods and services belong to output.

Goods and services are considered part of the output if they are supplied to units other than their producers (ESA, par. 3.08). That is why some activities and their goods or services are not recorded as production: for example, domestic services are produced and consumed within the same household. In this case, services (or goods in other cases) do not generate income, final consumption expenditure, and employment. These human products are not 'socially' produced and consumed, that is, are not collective goods and services or exchanged through the market, or donated for free or at no market prices (*i.e.* supplied to other households). These products are produced and consumed internally in the households.

In addition to the goods and services offered through the market (disposed of on the market or intended to be disposed of), therefore at an economically significant price (market price) to other IUs, within the production boundary of the economy, the following shall be recorded as well (ESA, par. 1.29):

- Production of individual and collective services by government;
- Own-account production of housing services by owner-occupiers;
- Production of goods for own final consumption, *e.g.* of agricultural products;
- Own-account construction, including the one by households;
- Production of services by paid domestic staff;
- Breeding of fish in fish farms;
- Production forbidden by law, as long as all units involved in the transaction enter into it voluntarily;
- Production from which the revenues are not declared in full to the fiscal authorities, *e.g.* clandestine production of textiles.

The following fall outside the production boundary, and shall not be recorded in the ESA (ESA, par. 1.30):

- Domestic and personal services produced and consumed within the same household, *e.g.* cleaning, the preparation of meals, or the care of sick or elderly people;
- Volunteer services that do not lead to the production of goods, *e.g.* care-taking and cleaning without payment;
- Natural breeding of fish in open seas.

It is clear that human-produced goods and services supplied outside the market are considered into the output if they are 'socially' produced by IUs (government or non-profit institutions) and supplied to other IUs. Products of self-production for self-consumption are considered only in some cases (own-account constructions, the development of software and mineral exploration, housing services, agricultural and other products for own final consumption). On these products, there is a parallel market in the economy, and goods are involved in addition to work. That is why also volunteer activities that produce goods are included: Examples of such activities are the construction of a dwelling, church or other building (ESA, par. 3.08).

Productions for own inputs of productions (intermediate consumption), in a vertically integrated production system, and other self-produced services for self-consumption internally in IUs are excluded. With this approach to output, several important domestic services produced by households themselves are excluded (ESA, par. 3.09):

- Cleaning, decoration, and maintenance of the dwelling as far as these activities are also common for tenants;
- Cleaning, servicing, and repair of household durables;
- Preparation and serving of meals;
- Care, training, and instruction of children;
- Care of sick, infirm, or old people;
- Transportation of members of the household or their goods.

Finally, there are goods and services produced with the ancillary activities, that is supporting activity undertaken within an enterprise in order to enable the principal or secondary activities of local KAUs to be carried out (ESA, par. 3.12).

Also, the outputs of ancillary activities in the IUs shall not be considered and recorded, except that there is an establishment undertaking only ancillary activities, there is at least one employee, and it is even better if there is a separate accountancy, and it is at the end statistically observable (ESA, par. 1.31).

In conclusion, we recall that output is part of the total resources of the economy (with imports), available to satisfy the needs of uses of goods and services (intermediate and final consumption, changes in inventories, gross fixed capital formation, acquisitions less disposals of valuables and exports) (ESA, par. 1.116). Not all human useful goods and services are included in output but only those whose production is included in the production boundary.

Measurement of Output and Conventions

Several conventions and ad-hoc measurement solutions are introduced to statistically measure output that can affect the level of output.

"The first account in the sequence of ESA accounts is the production account, which records the output of the production process" (ESA, par. 1.119).

Goods and services included in output are valued in terms of money and, specifically for market output, they are valued at economically significant prices (market prices). Valuation at different prices is possible and is considered in ESA.

Some conventions are adopted by ESA for valuations (ESA, par. 1.33) concerning the following disaggregation of output:

- Government output;
- Output of insurance services and financial intermediation services indirectly measured;
- Collective services provided by the government as final consumption expenditure and not as intermediate consumption.

The valuation of IUs output is so different with respect to specific sub-populations of units, based on their specific data availability: sample surveys, administrative data, and micro-economic accounts.

Transactions are economic flows that arise as an interaction between institutional units by mutual agreement: transactions in products describe the origin (domestic output or imports) of products (ESA, par. 1.66).

However, the ESA 2010 system records some actions within institutional units as transactions (because the unit is operating in two different capacities). The purpose of recording these intra-unit transactions is to give a more analytically useful picture of output, final uses, and costs (ESA, par. 1.67).

All own-produced output used for final uses within the same institutional unit shall be recorded. Own-produced output used for intermediate consumption within the same institutional unit shall be recorded only when production and intermediate consumption take place in different local KAUs within the same institutional unit. Output produced and used as intermediate consumption within the same local KAU shall not be recorded (ESA, par. 1.69).

Furthermore, the assignment of output to a specific section is approximated by attributing the total value of the output of an IU to its prevailing economic activity, even if one or more economic activities can be carried out by the same unit.

To make more precise the classification of output, at the micro-unit level, ESA has introduced a subdivision of IUs into more homogeneous sub-units in terms of organization, economic activity and so of output: the local kind-of-activity units (local KAUs). They are grouped into industries based on their type of activity, at the class level (four digits) of the NACE Rev. 2 (Eurostat, 2008: 15, 40); an activity that is characterized by an input of products, a production process and an output of products (ESA, par. 1.56).

Lastly, the timing of recording is when the goods or services are produced and not when paid for by a purchaser (ESA, par. 1.102).

Unobserved Economy

National accounts offices attempt to provide an exhaustive measure of production, Output, GDP, and other aggregates of the economy, observed and left unobserved, and also covering products that are non-directly observed in statistical surveys or administrative files. Best practices to measure unobserved economies have been provided by international organizations (OECD, 2002). Shadow economy is an important non-observed component (Schneider *et al.*, 2000).

This part of the output can be extremely important for the vitality and resilience in the long run of the economy allowing sustainability: we think about the large number of small producers, a widespread phenomenon in many economies and regions.

In the context of Italian economic accounting, various techniques are used successfully to estimate non-observed productive activities (Calzaroni, 2000; Pascarella *et al.*, 2000; Quintano *et al.*, 2008).

This component accounted for more than 10% of the Italian GDP in 2018 (Istat, 2020).

Classification and Reclassification of Output

Standard international classifications of Output are introduced by the UN and EU manual starting from the base definition of 'market' items. This statistical framework plays a central role in the Institutional Units (IUs) classified as 'market', for their engagement in transactions of products at 'economically significant prices' (and so-called 'market transactions') with other IUs (mainly corporations, households, government, and non-profit institutions).

ESA 2010, specifically, introduced specific criteria to define market output with respect to previous ESA editions, to ensure a uniform approach (ESA, par. 1.50).

Produced goods and services included in Output are generated by specific economic activities, classified and linked in statistical classifications. For example, considering what is called the "green" economy (Pizzoli, 2020), several of the producible goods and services can be identified as 'preferable' products for their environmental impact throughout their life cycle (ISO, 2018). These products imply, by definition, a reduction of human impact on nature, at the time of production or consumption, with respect to other products produced (UN, 2014). Their productions identify industries and economic activities that have environmental positive effects concerning environmental protection and natural resources management (Eurostat, 2001b, 2014a). In Italy, the component of environmental goods and services is estimated to be about 2% of the total output and growing faster than the rest of the economy (Istat, 2021).

Furthermore, goods and services are mainly produced by corporations and non-profit institutions (serving households and corporations) for individual (final and intermediate) consumption (individual goods and services) (ESA, par. 2.45). The general government sector (S.13) produces the non-market output intended for individual and, in particular, collective consumption (collective goods and services) (ESA, par. 2.111).

This statistical link between products in the Output and units ('institutional units' in the SNA and ESA system), allows a recalculation of sub-systems of accounts to specific target sub-populations of statistical units; for example, the specific system of non-profit institutions and market units that belong to the Third or Social Economy (TSE) sector (UNSTAT, 2018). At the moment, in the EU the components of IUs serving households are annually estimated.

CONCLUSION

GDP measures mainly market transactions. Several products without a market transaction are excluded or non-observed and will be useful to have a measure for sustainability analysis.

Furthermore, GDP ignores critical dimensions and development aspects such as social costs, environmental impacts, and income inequality. A more comprehensive and systemic view of development can be produced by expanding national accounts.

Still further information can be extracted from core national accounts aggregates, as Output, for analysis, policymakers' support, and monitoring of development policies results. Several manuals are available from UNSD, OECD, and ESA. There are promising examples of implementations and the work is in progress. Further studies from researchers and national accounts specialists are necessary to integrate results, speed up statistical supply and produce important synergies in a fast-running, and changing globalized world.

CHAPTER 10

Public Spending, Multinational De-Localization and Income Redistribution: The Budget Trap for Policymakers Toward Sustainable Development Policies

Edoardo Pizzoli[1,*]

[1] *Department of Finance, University of Luxembourg, Luxembourg, Luxembourg*

Abstract: The growing awareness of the need for sustainable development at the United Nations level, has highlighted the complexity of system dynamics and the challenges for governments and policymakers. New objectives, based on increasing dimensions considered relevant to sustainability, are incorporated in the agenda of policy designers: in this scenario, the traditional economic goals of long-term prosperity become more difficult to achieve.

Moreover, although governments in Europe, the United States, and many other market economy countries are committed to balancing the public budget, de facto, public deficits are realized every year and public debt accumulates. Specifically in the EU, due to the pandemic crisis, the previously agreed limits of the public deficit in relation to the level of economic activity are currently not respected. The data and statistical trends are evident.

In the current organization of the globalized economy, multinational groups do not help the public authorities in governing the economy, playing as autonomous economic entities. The introduction of technological innovations and the re-location of plants to deal with regional demand crises, falling prices, and global market competition worsen the tasks of economic and social stabilization. Shareholders demand profitability and, consequently, private financial statements must be annually positive.

This is a budget 'trap': policymakers struggle with income redistribution to address the current economic crisis. This dilemma is discussed with examples from OECD countries.

Keywords: Fiscal policy, Financial sustainability, Government spending, Public sector accounting, Public budget, Public deficit, Public debt.

* **Corresponding author Edoardo Pizzoli:** Department of Finance, Department of Finance, University of Luxembourg, Luxembourg, Luxembourg; E-mail: edoardo.pizzoli@uni.lu

INTRODUCTION

The adoption of the new paradigm of sustainable development at several geographical and policy governance levels, with the effort to include in a single frame environmental - socio-economic objectives, has highlighted issues already known in the past such as the complexity of the social system dynamics and the limits of our policy instruments.

A specific perspective will be adopted to address the issue of sustainability in this paper: that of the budgets in the system of economic accounts. How to keep economic sustainability within a sustainable development framework?

The recent explosion of the debt mechanism and the governments' reactions will be introduced in the first part. Considerations on the context of market globalisation will pave the way for a reflection on the "budget trap" and the possible developments for economic theory and policy practice in the conclusions.

General Government Spending and Public Debt

Government spending or expenditure in the National Accounts includes all government compensation of employees, intermediate and final consumption, investment (capital expenditure), interests, and transfer payments (social benefits, incentives, and redistribution items) (UNSTAT, 2009; Eurostat, 2013).

In government finance accounting, the acquisition of goods and services for current use by governments, to directly satisfy the individual or collective needs of the community, is classed as Government Final Consumption Expenditure (GFCE); while the government acquisition of goods and services intended to create "future benefits", such as infrastructure investment or research spending, is classed as government investment (Government Gross Capital Formation, GGCF). These two main types of government spending, on final consumption and gross capital formation, together constitute one of the major components of Gross Domestic Product (GDP) (Eurostat, 2019c).

Internally to the public budget, given the budget constraint, there is a competition between expenditure components, specifically on items supporting environmental and social sustainability with respect to doubtful or even "destructive" expenses like, for example, military weapons systems.

This is a major instrument of policy at the national level. As we know, there is also a concern about this main economic aggregate as there is an annual push to expand and redistribute this collective spending.

Public debt, sometimes also referred to as government debt, represents the total outstanding debt (bonds and other securities) of a country's central government. As we know, public debt can be raised both externally and internally, where external debt is the debt owed to lenders outside the country and internal debt represents the government's obligations to domestic lenders.

Public debt is an important source of resources for a government to finance public spending and fill holes in the budget. Public debt as a percentage of GDP is usually used as an indicator of the ability of a government to meet its future obligations.

In 2019, before the Covid-19 pandemic crisis, the public debt situation at the global level was the following (Fig. **1**):

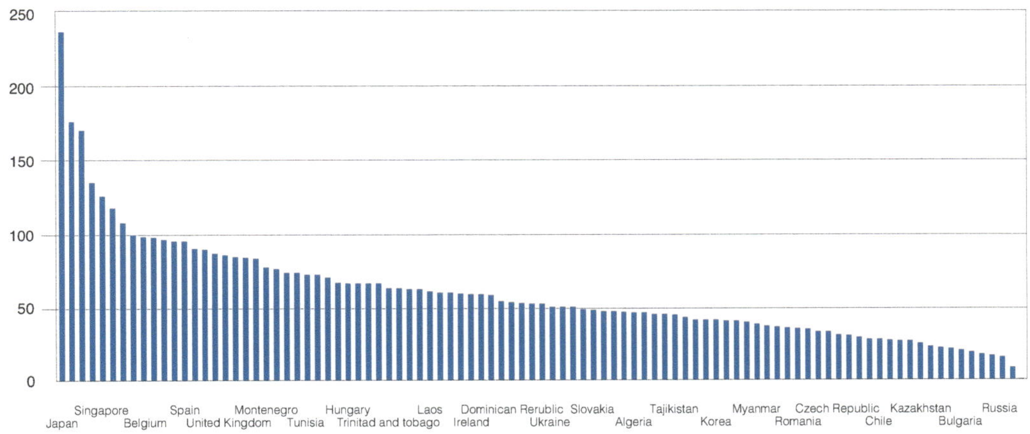

Fig. (1). Public debt (% of GDP) – Year 2019 (Source: UNSTAT).

In 2019, on available data, we had Japan with more than 200% debt, ten countries (USA, Italy, Greece, *etc.*) with more than 100% public debt, more than 50 countries with more than 50% debt, (we have to remember that not all the countries data are available or reliable; for example, it is estimated that Venezuela has overcome 300% of GDP.

The United States has the largest national debt in fiscal terms, while Japan has the largest relative debt of any other developed economy when compared to GDP.

After the Pandemic period, started at the end of 2019 with a new wave of economic crisis, this percentage exploded in most countries.

Public Deficit and Debt from 2020

General government deficit is defined as the negative balance of income and expenditure of government, including capital income and capital expenditures. In correspondence with the deficit, there is a "net borrowing" which means the government requires financial resources from other sectors.

This indicator is measured as a percentage of GDP. All OECD countries compile their data according to the 2008 System of National Accounts (UNSTAT, 2009).

Last OECD data on public deficit indicate increasing high levels in this negative budget balance (Fig. **2**):

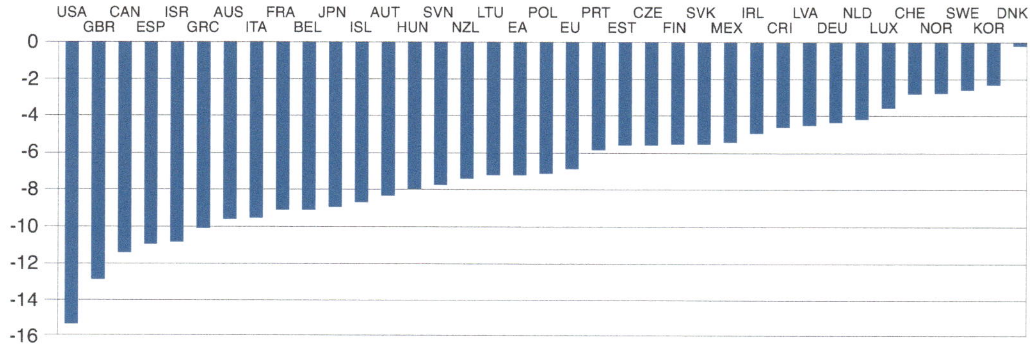

Fig. (2). General government deficit, total, % of GDP – Year 2020 (Source: OECD Data).

The North Atlantic countries (US, Canada, and UK) lead the negative budget ranking, followed by Israel, Australia, Japan, and other EU countries (Spain, Greece, Italy, France, Belgium, Austria, Hungary, *etc.*).

As a result of the pandemic crisis and the increased deficits, global debt (which includes corporate and household debt) rose by 28 percentage points to 256% of GDP, in 2020, according to the latest update of the IMF's Global Debt Database (Mbaye et al., 2018). We observed the largest one-year debt surge since World War II, with global debt rising to $226 trillion.

The value of only government debt worldwide was $87.4 US trillion, or 99% measured as a share of gross domestic product (GDP). Government debt accounted for almost 40% of all debt, the highest share since the 1960s.

The rise in government debt since 2007 is largely attributable to the global financial crisis of 2007–2008 and the last Covid-19 pandemic (Gaspar, 2021; IMF, 2022).

The Government's debt situation in 2020 is the following (Fig. **3**):

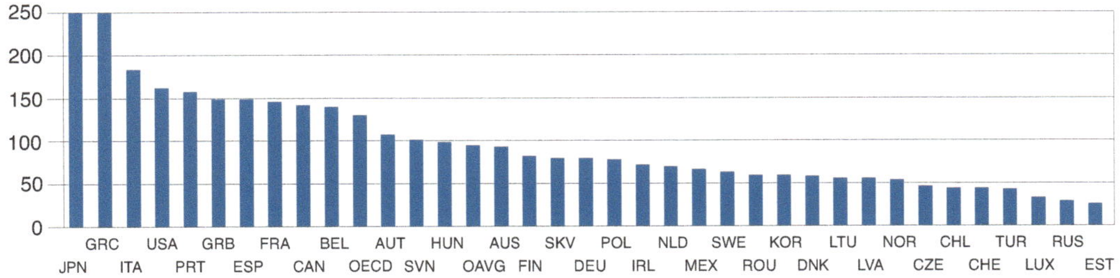

Fig. (3). General government debt, total, greater than 50% of GDP – Year 2020 (or latest available) (Source: OECD Data).

It is evident that debt increases are particularly strong in advanced economies (such as Japan, Italy, the US, France, *etc.*), where public debt rose from around 70% of GDP, in 2007, to 124% of GDP, in 2020. Private debt, on the other hand, rose at a more moderate rate from 164 to 178% of GDP, in the same period.

The global total debt trend since 1970, estimated by IMF, is the following (Fig. **4**):

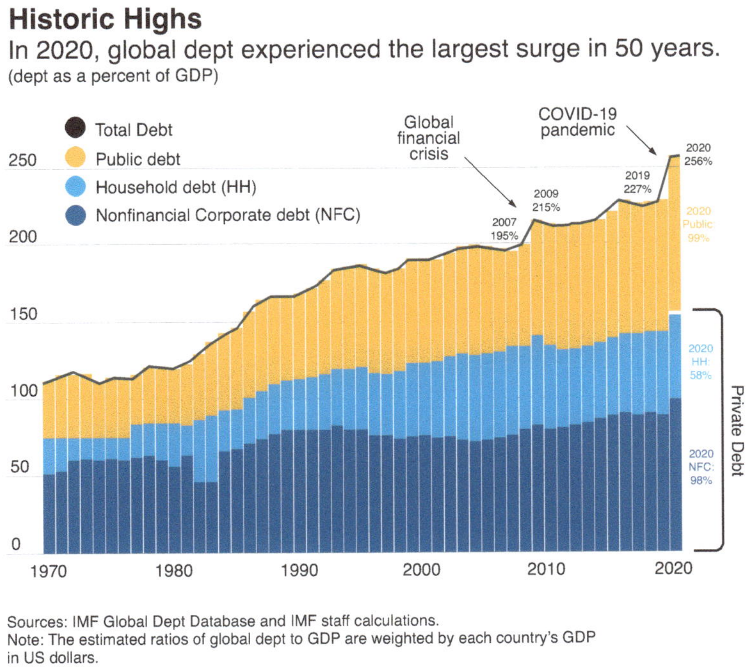

Fig. (4). Global total debt (% of GDP) – Year 2020 (Source: IMF).

Time series forecasts suggest that this tendency will continue in the coming years, without a possible external shock that induces a structural brake.

Japan Case: Fiscal Policy and Sustainability

The Japanese economy is an interesting case among the developed economies. The government offered several stimulus packages to boost economic recovery in an effort to soften the economic fallout from the coronavirus pandemic, with about 300 trillion JPY in direct fiscal spending. The action was to go towards supporting the economy and investors, with three main pillars, namely structural reforms: measures to prevent the spread of COVID-19, strengthening the healthcare system, and increased funding for natural disaster resilience. Of the three pillars, around 70% of the total budget went towards structural reforms that aim to transform the post-COVID-19 economy, particularly by promoting digitalization and green initiatives—both key policy areas for the government. Furthermore, this policy provided a “Go to Travel” subsidy scheme and further subsidy measures to support demand, with additional public works spending, and inducing corporate fixed investment in the previous national priority areas.

As a result of this fiscal policy, the forecast of the fiscal deficit will continue to be high in 2021 and 2022 (over 8.0% of GDP).

The Japanese government is currently spending around half of its total tax revenue on servicing its high debt; despite this, in 2022, the yield on 10-year Japanese bonds remains at a “surprisingly” low level at under 1 percent.

Within developed and industrialized countries is avant-garde in this choice, experimenting effects especially on economic sustainability, with this pushed public intervention on its economy while remaining in a market economy constraint. The risks are well known: loss of government credibility, short-term market price instability on public bonds, the explosion of the spread in interest rates, and, eventually, accounting default. That is the so-called “sovereign risk”, the potential that a nation's government will default on its “sovereign” debt by failing to meet its interest or principal payments.

This debt surge amplifies economic vulnerabilities, especially if financing conditions tighten. At the same time, high debt levels constrain the ability of the governments to support the recovery and the capacity of the private sector to invest in the medium term.

Japan's economic policy success, or failure, will only be visible in the medium-long run. On this base, we can evaluate the economic sustainability of this policy. From a short-run perspective, we can only see the immediate positive effects.

MULTINATIONALS AND DE-LOCALIZATION

Multinational companies (MNCs) as a corporate organization that owns and controls the production of goods or services in at least one country other than its home country, are dominating present global markets. Control is considered an important aspect of an MNC, to distinguish them from international portfolio investment organizations, such as some international mutual funds that invest in corporations abroad simply seeking ever-higher profits and to diversify their financial risks.

MNCs are organized as transnational groups that reallocate their assets and sites geographically with respect to their corporate policy of keeping profitability at the market levels, gaining new market shares, lowering labour and production costs, granting raw material sources, and keeping control of technologies and products to supply. In this process, MNCs are becoming more and more stateless or behaving as a government, with similar budget levels.

That is why the de-localisation and continuous re-localization of their establishment, in different parts of the country of origin or other areas of the world, has become part of their normal corporate strategy. Typically, nowadays, a State in the US or a member country in the EU is the location for the legal site (holding company) with strategic assets (for example, legal offices); a fiscal site is in a lower tax demanding country (a "fiscal paradise"); production is distributed in several developing countries (for example, for EU companies, in central-eastern Europe and China). Value added are concentrated and re-emerge in a friendly tax system.

With this approach of MNCs, the goods and services associated with consumption are becoming less local and increasingly externally sourced in geographical terms.

With economic de-localization, there is a transfer of activities, capital, and employment in areas that have competitive advantages. The result is "separated" geographical areas; head office sites (North America and Western Europe), raw materials sources' regions, transformation products areas, and consummation countries.

Public Policy and Attempts of Redistribution

The previously described evolution in the production and financial sectors had a heavy effect on the public balance: the effective possibility of financing expenses with taxation on the private sector (on companies and households) and the redistribution of resources with transfers. Tax and subsidies are the main instruments for fiscal policy to achieve income redistribution in society, which includes the transfer of income and wealth (including physical property) from some individuals to others through a social mechanism, typically on an economy-wide basis, rather than between selected individuals.

If the tax base of taxation is reduced, the resources to finance the necessary public expenditure are reduced. The national governments struggle (or make deals) with MNCs and compete with each other to keep fiscal sites or relevant strategic activities.

The result is a "budget game" between the two competing economic players.

CONCLUSION

The "budget constraint" reminds us of a basic human rule that non-renewable resources are limited in space and time, even if we know that the financial resources can be created in practice, mainly by issuing money and with the mechanism of banking multiplication of deposits.

Economists and financial analysts suggest that governments should find the right "balance": the crucial challenge of mixing fiscal and monetary policies, weighting social and economic needs.

In the private sector, multinational groups strike to satisfy the financial market constraint of an annual budget surplus, and the imperative of shareholders, competing each other and with Governments to reduce taxes.

The question is which is the "red line" for expenditure and debt that governments should never cross before a possible financial meltdown? This is the nightmare of all policymakers; they fill in the trap as, in reality, nobody knows the limit.

We could say that, according to what the economic theory tells us, a robust fundamental productive economy is necessary to support new expenses and the weight of debts. Economic sustainability, in the long run, comes back to the surface as one of the conditions for the sustainable development of society. Different is a financial constraint, that with a numerical "consistency" could be extended to satisfy further "real" objectives of society, systemic changes, and human development. This is without losing its purpose as a powerful tool of control for efficient economic programming.

The leading economics in the world on these policies will show us the way.

CHAPTER 11

The Green Economy: A Possible Technological Option to Deal with Economic Un-Sustainability

Edoardo Pizzoli[1,*]

[1] *Department of Finance, University of Luxembourg, Luxembourg, Luxembourg*

Abstract: The global economic crises of the new century are long-lasting and seem without prospects of recovery. The 'green' economy paradigm proposes an alternative basket of products with respect to the standard one, currently available for consumption and investment in the industrial economies of the 21st century.

The green economy is proposed as a smart solution for an alternative growth path that should lead to sustainable economic development.

If this is a possible scenario, a specific sustainability accounting system is necessary. This system should allow us to investigate: whether the available policy instruments are sufficient to achieve the required structural change in the economy and if the economic transition will take place in time with respect to what scientific studies require.

This new paradigm and the related economic trends are discussed in this chapter.

Keywords: Economic crisis, Economic sustainability, Green conversion, Green economy, Long-term trends, Technological progress.

INTRODUCTION

The present chapter raises several questions related to the possible evolution of the economic crisis in the current economic and political context. What seems emerging as new in the mainstream attempt to govern the difficulties involved, is the proposal of the so-called 'green' economy and the linked sustainable development policy strategy. This is evident in actual EU policy strategy by the European Commission and documents published by UN agencies.

[*] **Corresponding author Edoardo Pizzoli:** Department of Finance, University of Luxembourg, Luxembourg, Luxembourg; E-mail: edoardo.pizzoli@uni.lu

In the following paragraphs, a brief introduction to the argument is provided to address some of the critical issues that should be investigated by economic research in the future.

WHAT IS A GREEN ECONOMY?

'What and how to produce' into the economy are the canonical questions for economic science and normally the answer is based on basic human needs, consumerism, enterprises' supply of commodities to the market, and political choices. To find out which possible options are currently available, it is necessary to get inside the black box of the production technologies at the specific historical time (Rosenberg, 1983). Going backward from final consumption to the origin of the production chains of the economy, several of the producible goods and services can be identified as 'preferable' products for their environmental impact throughout their life cycle (ISO, 2018). These products imply, by definition, a reduction of human impact on nature, at the time of production or consumption, with respect to other products currently produced (UN, 2014). Their productions identify industries and economic activities that have environmental positive effects concerning environmental protection and natural resources management (Eurostat, 2001b, 2014a).

The 'green' economy proposes this basket of 'green' products to be produced in alternative with respect to the standard one that is currently offered in industrial economies. This is a perspective of a structural change in the economy that implies a different growth path and, as a result, an alternative economic development scenario at the world level.

New Economic Policy Perspective for a Green Conversion

At the international level in the last decades, after important climate changes and scientific results, there was a growing consensus on the need to transform the world economy to reduce CO_2 emissions and natural resource degradation.

Examples of international policy actions, grown after several international meetings, are the UNEP Green Economy Initiative (UNEP, 2017), the OECD Project on Green Growth (OECD, 2011), and the European Commission's commitment to move towards a green economic policy (Eurostat, 2023; EEA, 2018).

As UNEP says on its homepage, "We promote the transition to economies that are low carbon, resource-efficient ...an alternative to today's dominant economic model. Over the past decade, the concept of the green economy has emerged as a strategic priority for many governments" (www.unenvironment.org).

Many and an increasing number of countries, regions, and, at the local level, urban and rural administrations are implementing plans or single actions to contribute to a green conversion. This seems to be a historical trend at the beginning of the 21st century.

A Missing History of Green Technologies

Technologies, as already largely documented, had a historical evolution across the different eras of human development with some important jumps and acceleration that allows, even if arbitrary, a division in phases (Buchanan, 2018). They are characterized by the dominant materials and sources of power of the period, and their application to production.

An enormous acceleration of Western technological development has characterized the recent centuries. Specifically, since the eighteenth century producers and scientists have become systematically linked, this has allowed technology to flourish (Mokir, 2008).

Nowadays technology is intended as the utilization of natural phenomena and regularities for human purposes. In practice, this allowed humanity to develop over time systematic techniques for making and doing things, all of them having some kind of impact on the environment. Despite this necessary consequence, some of the products are preferable compared to others for their reduced impact throughout their life cycle (UN, 2014). These products can be labeled as 'green' and they should allow defining 'green' or 'greener technologies' in a geographical region at a specific historical time.

Unfortunately, there is no history of green technologies and it is unknown if they have evolved towards a lower environmental impact throughout human civilizations. What is known is that the market, together with geopolitical choices, has been the driver of changes at least since the first industrial revolution in Britain. Some technologies have been preferred in enterprises' investments for their capacity to reduce costs and increase labour productivity, regardless of the negative externalities to the environment or human health. Relative prices are the regulator and driving of business choices, so cheaper technologies were preferred if that allowed companies to be more competitive on the market and to produce higher profits.

Currently, science proposes some solutions that could be greener than those actually used if relative prices would change in the market and policymakers decide to intervene.

Changing Technologies Allows Sustainability?

Based on the previous perspective and the possibilities available to present societies, different scenarios can be foreseen and many questions arise. The first question is: can be possible to find a solution to an actual global crisis going into the black box of production possibilities of the economies and changing the production set? Is a green economy a smart solution for an alternative growth path that allows also sustainable economic development?

A field of economic research, starting from the academic teaching and publications of Schumpeter, identified in technology the critical dimension of economic change (Schumpeter, 1911). Technological innovation can drive the economy 'possibly to growth', anyhow to business cycles. The long-run sustainability of the economy and eventually of its development depends on many factors and there is no guarantee that a conversion toward greener technologies will allow such a result. Furthermore, the issue of sustainability can be seen from different points of view.

A shift in the production bundle of the economy could be a technological solution to the 'environmental sustainability' problem but maybe not a solution to the 'economic sustainability' in capitalistic-based economies. Changing productions and technologies involved can create new occasions for business and revitalize a depressed economy in the short run. New and more efficient products and productions substitute previous ones, stimulating further research and development and industrial applications. A substitution effect can revitalize the economy through renovated final consumption and investment of products. Supply will create demand. Capitals will move to the new promising sectors of the economy keeping high the profits and investments.

The drawback to this scenario is the crisis in industries and geographical areas where the non-green productions are based. Unemployment is expected with the introduction of new, normally labour-saving, technologies. A reorganization of production among old and new companies, factories, and geographical areas is involved in stimulating capital, materials, and human mobility.

What will be the net effect of this process of development? The overall process of technological innovation and reorganization of the economy will be sufficient to find out a durable solution to recurrent difficulties of capital valorisation? Financial capital and the international financial system can find stability if policymakers and key economic players persist in this direction (Duménil *et al*, 2006)? This is an open question that requires a further effort of economic investigation to give an answer to the sustainability issue.

Conversion to the Green Economy or Barbarism?

The analyses of environmental transformation from a scientific point of view present a catastrophic scenario and it would seem that there are few policy choices available. Furthermore, the speed at which political mechanisms react to the changes and the economic system responds to existing policies is very slow.

For example, the Intergovernmental Panel on Climate Change (IPCC) reports that we are in an ecological emergency and, if the scientists' forecasts are true, a great collective effort is required, always if it is still possible to reverse the trend of climate change (IPCC, 2023). As is known, global warming is at the base of changes, generated mainly by the greenhouse effect that was produced by the emission of CO2 into the atmosphere. This, in turn, was produced by the combustion of oil and other fossil fuels: the anthropic cause (the human activities of production and consumption) of the rise in temperature has been widely underestimated. A few degrees of rising earth temperature trigger final devastating reactions on the entire biodiversity (IPCC, 2019).

Are we moving rapidly towards global chaos? Evidence would seem to confirm.

The economic system and the actual technologies of production have to be rapidly revised to stop or even reduce the increase in temperature. The international policy effort has been put in place with the Paris Agreement (2018) but, beyond technical difficulties, there is still no full agreement on coordination and collective-individual actions to take.

Lastly, mass consensus on the transition toward an alternative economy has still a long way to go. Will we, as a whole, be able to react on time?

EU EFFORT TOWARDS A CONVERSION TO THE GREEN ECONOMY: RESULTS AND PROSPECTIVE

The EU under the European Commission policy initiative is engaged to reach several long-run objectives of sustainable development and green economy conversion.

The Environmental Action Plan (EAP) started in the '70s. The last 8th EAP in 2022, spans to 2050 and has a long-term goal to reach 'well-being and a resilient society within ecological limits'. The underlying strategy is the transition to the Circular Economy, which is based on sustainable management of natural resources, biodiversity protection, resource efficiency (with a green and low-carbon economy), and technological innovations.

Main EU member countries had a leading role at the UN policy level at least since the UN Conference on Environment and Development (Rio Earth Summit) in 1992 where the first comprehensive action plan to build a global partnership for sustainable development was set (Agenda 21) and the Commission on Sustainable Development (CSD) was established. During Prodi Commission (1999 -2004), the UN approved the Millennium Development Goals (MDGs), at the 2000 Millennium Summit and the plan of implementation on sustainable development, at the 2002 World Summit. In 2011, the EU achieved an enhanced participation status in the UN General Assembly and, in 2012, during the second Barroso Commission (2010-2014) the third Rio Conference on Sustainable Development took place. Finally, it was during the Junker Commission (2014-2019) and the last von der Leyen Commission that the EU initiative accelerated, fully adopting the UN 2030 Agenda for sustainable development.

As a legal base, the entry into force of key EU Treaties (Maastricht 1993, Amsterdam 1999, and Lisbon 2009) introduced chapters and specific policy objectives on sustainable development, laying the foundations for present European policies.

A combination of action plans and instruments have been adopted by the European Commission to reach these objectives: the latest initiatives have been the new Circular Economy Action Plan (CEAP) 2020, Investment Plan for Europe (from the 2015 Junker Plan), several European Directives, further legislative actions, and information campaigns. An InvestEU program is already planned for 2021 – 2027 and a re-launch of policies is foreseen by the European Commission.

All interventions were carried out within the framework, generally shared by all European Commissions in the last decades, of enlargement of the European market and liberalization of trade and investments. Trade-induced growth actually adds pressure to the environment and can lead to unsustainable production patterns; that is why environmental policies were gradually implemented but, always, respecting the free market approach. In this context, the system of enterprises (national and multinationals) clearly has a key role to play and a responsibility in ensuring that their activities positively contribute to sustainable development and green economy conversion.

Data available from Eurostat DB show the results of European policies in this direction (Fig. **1**):

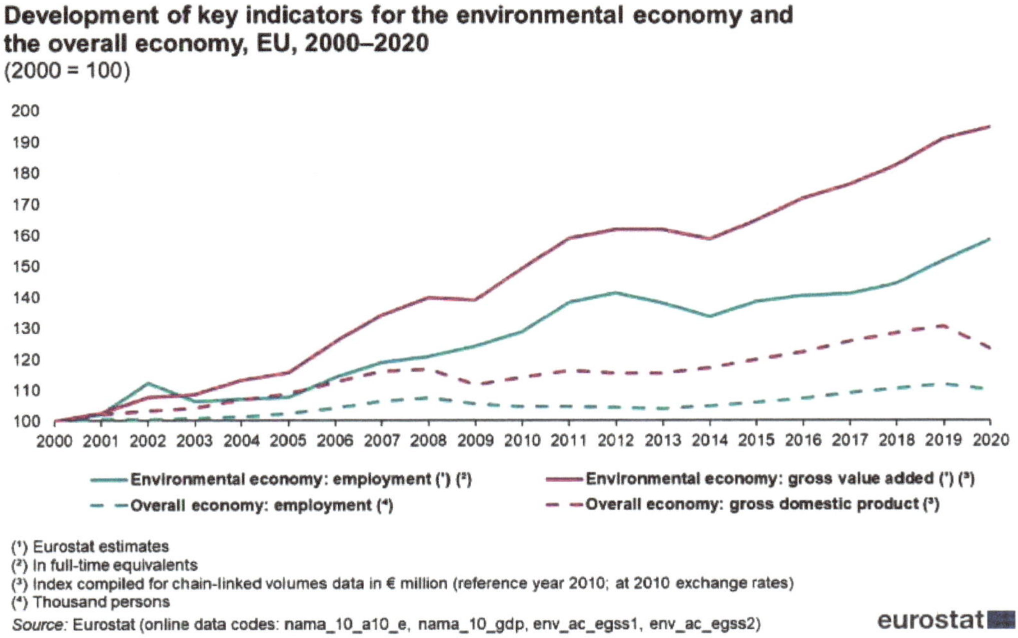

Fig. (1). EU economy trends.

Between 2000 and 2020, value-added and employment in the EU environmental economy grew faster than in the overall economy. Employment and value-added in the EU environmental economy continued to grow in 2020 even though the overall economy contracted. Total gross value added grew by 1.9%, contributing 2.0% to the GDP of the European Union. In the same period, overall employment grew by 4.5%, whereas overall employment decreased by 1.4% and EU gross domestic product fell by 5.7%. About 55% of environmental gross value added and employment is related to environmental goods and services sold or intended to be sold on the market; the remainder stems from output produced for own use (ancillary or final) or for non-market purposes (as give-away for free or at non-significant prices). Considering only market output (note that reporting is mandatory for EU member countries only on market output of the environmental economy), gross value added grew a bit faster but contributed less to the EU-wide market GDP.

Output and gross value-added dynamics show some significant differences when considered by sector of activity (Table **1**).

Table 1. Index of annual variations output by NACE activities, 2007 - 2020.

NACE activities	Output	
	Mean	**Max**
Total - all NACE activities	**103.2**	**110.4**
Agriculture, forestry and fishing	106.8	117.7
Mining and quarrying; manufacturing	101.4	120.6
Construction	103.7	117.2
Services	104.0	112.3
Electricity, gas, steam and air conditioning supply; water supply; sewage, waste management and remediation activities	101.8	109.3

Primary sectors, services, and construction had the highest average dynamics in the period 2007 – 2020 with respectively +6.8%, +4.0%, and +3.7% for output. Manufacturing, mining, and other sub-sectors were slower than the total average of +3.2%.

At the previously measured speed, even recognizing the better performance of the green economy compared to the total economy, the EU policy targets will be reached very slowly and far away in the future.

With an annual rate of growth of around +3% and assuming a full substitution effect of the actual non-environmental output (*i.e.* based on non-renewable energy and with high carbon emissions) with environmental one, the green economy will double in 20 years, that is in 2040, reaching only a 4% level of the actual European economy (Fig. **2**). In 2050, the green economy will be only 2.7 times higher and 5.6% of the total economy; it will take about a century to increase 20 times and, lastly, 130 years will be necessary for a complete replacement of the conventional economy (in 2150).

This actual rate of replacement driven by the market and with market-oriented policies, seems quite ineffective with respect to the transition objective of the economy. To reach a conversion in the desired timing, the annual rate of growth should be similar to that experienced in the past by wartime or planned socialist economies. With +10% of annual growth starting from 2020, the environmental output will double in 8 years, in 2028, and a complete replacement will be in about 38 years, in 2058; whereas with a rate of +20%, this timing would be almost half (double in 2024 and replacement in 2041).

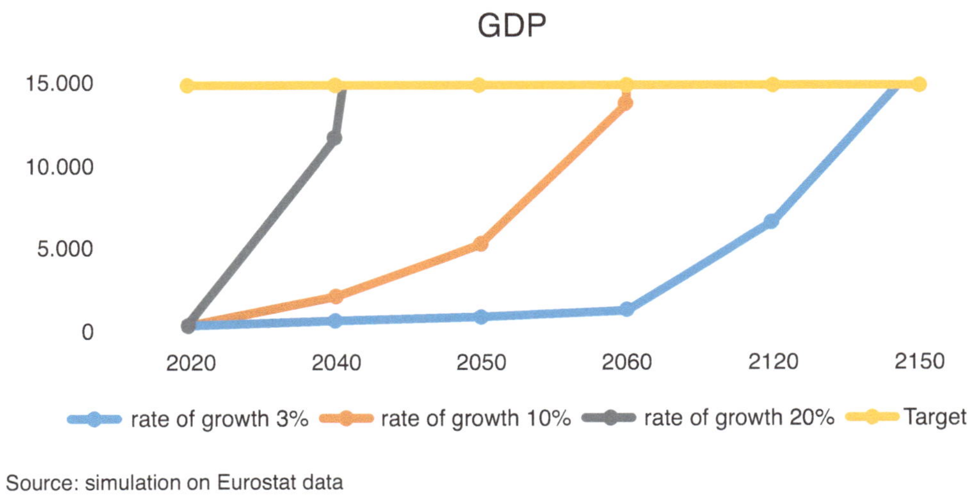

Fig. (2). EU GDP (billion EUR), 2020 - 2150. Source: simulation on Eurostat data.

Only in some peak years, of high global economic growth and highly stimulating policies, and in some specific economic activities, a rate of growth of a scale between +10% and +20% reached in Europe (see Table **1**). That means that instability of growth over time and an average low rate of growth are the norm in the last decade. These results raise a serious question about economic policy and instruments that should be used in the future in the EU.

CONCLUSION

Several questions have been identified in this chapter related to the proposed 'green' possibility as a way-out to global economy's persistent crises. Furthermore, the sustainability of the 'green' economy, from different points of view, seems uncertain. Given that the required technology change will work at the environmental level, will it be effective against the economic crisis? Which economic policy instruments should be used to reach the objective of this kind of economic transition? How to speed up the policy process that is already in the running?

The issues at the base of the questions are very demanding in terms of research while some policy proposals would be desirable.

A great effort of investigation will be necessary in the coming years to study the implications of such a possible change in the economic development model in the EU and, globally, in UN members' countries. Researchers wishing to find answers to the deriving questions have to join their efforts in a joint world research program.

This chapter is based on a paper presented by the author at World Economics Association (WEA) Conference "The 2008 Economic Crisis Ten Years On: In Retrospect, Context, and Prospect", 15 October – 30 November 2018.

REFERENCES

Bhanumati P. (2021). *India's Efforts in Enhancing the Consideration of Natural Capital*, ICASS Conference, Luxembourg. Available from: https://icaas.eu/papers.

Battellini F., Tudini A. (2021). *Integrated Framework for Monetary Environmental Accounts*, ICASS Conference, Luxembourg. Available from: https://icaas.eu/papers.

BEA (2020). *New Digital Economy Estimates*, Digital economy satellite account report, Washington. Available from: https://www.bea.gov/data/special-topics/digital-economy.

Buchanan, R.A. (2018). *History of Technology*, Encyclopædia Britannica, Chicago. Available from: www.britannica.com/technology/history-of-technology.

Calzaroni, M. (2000). *L'occupazione Come Strumento per la Stima Esaustiva del PIL e la Misura del Sommerso*, contributo al seminario dell'Istat "La nuova contabilità nazionale", Rome, Italy.

CII-ITC (2020). *Integrating Sustainability into Indian Supply Chains*, CESD, New Delhi. Available from: https://sustainabledevelopment.in/publications/.

Costanza, R., Kubiszewski, I., Giovannini, E., Lovins, H., McGlade, J., Pickett, K. E., Ragnarsdóttir, K. V., Robers, D., De Vogli, R. and Wilkinson, R. (2014). *Time to Leave GDP Behind*, Nature, Vol. 505, Macmillan Publishers, London.

Council of the EU (2015). *The Promotion of the Social Economy as a Key Driver of Economic and Social Development in Europe*, Council Conclusions, Brussels. Available from: https://data.consilium.europa.eu/doc/document/ST-15071-2015-INIT/en/pdf.

Duménil, G. and Lévy, D. (2006). *La Finance Capitaliste : Rapports de Production et Rapports de Classe*, in La Finance Capitaliste, Presses Universitaires de France, Paris. Available from: https://www.cepremap.fr/membres/dlevy/dle2006c.htm.

Dyball R. and Newell, B. (2015). *Understanding Human Ecology. A Systems Approach to Sustainability*, Routledge, London.

EC (2019). *Annual Sustainable Growth Strategy 2020*, 650 final, Brussels. Available from: https://ec.europa.eu/info/sites/default/files/2020-european-semester-annual-sustainable-growth-strategy_en.pdf.

EC (2020). *Farm-to-Fork Strategy. For a Fair, Healthy and Environmentally-Friendly Food System*, EU Green Deal, publication, Brussels. Available from: https://www.shrmonitor.org/european-farm-to-f-rk-strategy-in-the-time-of-food-security/?gad_source=1&gad_campaignid=15093706068&gbraid=0AAAAAB8VsFtHEKSzi2lyUYLOcvg7prEH_&gclid=CjwKCAiAj8LLBhAkEiwAJjbY79dKq7Tx9ojB24I-_wBhkdxa9iK2VpNX5hQZ92rOXRyqSKitkxaQRxoCB1kQAvD_BwE.

ECA (2016). *Is the Commission's System for Performance Measurement in Relation to Farmers' Incomes Well Designed and Based on Sound Data?*, Special Report No 1, Luxembourg. Available from: https://www.eca.europa.eu/sites/ep/en/Pages/Policy-areas.aspx.

Edwards, J. R. and Walker, S. P. (2021). *The Routledge Companion to Accounting History*, second edition, Routledge, Abingdon.

EEA (2018). *National Policies and Measures on Climate Change Mitigation in Europe in 2017*, Copenhagen.

Available from: www.eea.europa.eu.

EnviStats India (2018). *Supplement on Environment Accounts*, New Delhi. Available from: https://www.mospi.gov.in/web/mospi/reports-publications.

EnviStats India (2019-2022a). *Vol. I: Environment Statistics*, various years, New Delhi. Available from: https://www.mospi.gov.in/web/mospi/reports-publications.

EnviStats India (2019, 2022b). *Vol. II Environment Accounts*, various years New Delhi. Available from: https://www.mospi.gov.in/web/mospi/reports-publications.

ESS (2014). *ESS Vision 2020: Building the Future of European Statistics*, Luxemburg. Available from: https://ec.europa.eu/eurostat/.

EU (2004). *The Economic Accounts for Agriculture in the Community*, EAA, Regulation of the European Parliament and of the Council N. 138, Brussels. Available from: https://eur-lex.europa.eu/.

EU (2014). *Disclosure of non-Financial and Diversity Information by Certain Large Undertakings and Groups*, Directive of the European Parliament and of the Council N. 95, amending Directive 2013/34/EU, Brussels. Available from: https://eur-lex.europa.eu/.

EU (2018). *the European System of National and Regional Accounts in the European Union*, Commission Delegated Regulation, N. 280, amending Regulation (EC) No 138/2004 of the European Parliament and of the Council, Brussels. Available from: https://eur-lex.europa.eu/.

EU (2019). *Sustainability-Related Disclosures in the Financial Services Sector*, Regulation N. 2088 of the European Parliament and of the Council, Brussels. Available from: https://eur-lex.europa.eu/.

EU (2020). *Establishment of a Framework to Facilitate Sustainable Investment*, Regulation of the European Parliament and of the Council N. 852, amending Regulation (EU) No 2019/2088, Brussels. Available from: https://eur-lex.europa.eu/.

EU (2021a). *Environmentally Sustainable Economic Activities, and Specifying the Methodology to Comply with that Disclosure Obligation*, Commission Delegated Regulation, N. 2178, supplementing Regulation (EU) 2020/85, Brussels. Available from: https://eur-lex.europa.eu/.

EU (2021b). *European Environmental Economic Accounts*, SEEA, Regulation of the European Parliament and of the Council N. 691, Brussels. Available from: https://eur-lex.europa.eu/.

EU (2022a). *Corporate Sustainability Reporting*, Directive of the European Parliament and of the Council N. 2464, amending Regulation (EU) No 537/2014, Directive 2004/109/EC, Directive 2006/43/EC and Directive 2013/34/EU, Brussels. Available from: https://eur-lex.europa.eu/.

EU (2022b). *Regional economic accounts for agriculture*, Regulation of the European Parliament and the Council N. 590, amending Regulation (EC) No 138/2004, Brussels. Available from: https://eur-lex.europa.eu/.

Eurostat (2001a). *Manual on the economic accounts for agriculture and forestry EAA/EA 97*, Luxembourg. Available from: https://ec.europa.eu/eurostat/web/products-manuals-and-guidelines/-/KS-27-00-782.

Eurostat (2001b). *Classification of Environmental Protection Activities 2000 (CEPA 2000)*, Luxembourg. Available from: https://ec.europa.eu/eurostat/ramon/nomenclatures.

Eurostat (2003). *Household Production and Consumption – Proposal for a Methodology of Household Satellite Accounts*, Working Papers and Studies, Luxembourg. Available from: https://ec.europa.eu/eurostat/

web/products-statistical-working-papers/-/KS-CC-03-003.

Eurostat (2008). *NACE Rev. 2 - Statistical Classification of Economic Activities in the European Community*, Methodologies and Working Papers, Luxembourg. Available from: https://ec.europa.eu/eurostat/web/products-manuals-and-guidelines/-/ks-ra-07-015.

Eurostat (2013). *European System of Accounts - ESA 2010*, Theme: Economy and Finance, Collection: Manual and guidelines, Luxembourg. Available from: https://ec.europa.eu/eurostat/web/esa-2010.

Eurostat (2014a). *Classification of Resource Management Activities (CReMA)*, in Regulation (EU) No 538/2014, Luxembourg. Available from: https://eur-lex.europa.eu.

Eurostat (2014b). *Resource Management Expenditure Accounts (ReMEA) – draft guidelines*, Luxembourg. Available from: https://ec.europa.eu/eurostat/documents/1798247/6191545/1-Resource-management-expenditure-accounts---draft-guidelines-2014.pdf/.

Eurostat (2014c). *Physical Energy Flow Accounts (PEFA) Manual 2014*, Luxembourg. Available from: https://ec.europa.eu/eurostat/documents/1798247/6191537/PEFA-Manual-2014-v20140515.pdf.

Eurostat (2015a). *Manual for Air Emissions Accounts*, Luxembourg. Available from: https://ec.europa.eu/eurostat/web/products-manuals-and-guidelines/-/KS-GQ-15-009.

Eurostat (2015b). *Strategy for Agricultural Statistics for 2020 and Beyond*, Unit E-1: Agriculture and fisheries, Luxembourg. Available from: https://ec.europa.eu/eurostat/web/agriculture/methodology/strategy-beyond-2020.

Eurostat (2016a). *Environmental Goods and Services Sector Accounts — Handbook 2016 edition*, Luxembourg. Available from: https://ec.europa.eu/eurostat/web/products-manuals-and-guidelines/-/KS-GQ-16-008.

Eurostat (2016b). *Methodological Document on Labour Productivity Indicators for the EU-28: Quality Adjusted Labour Input*, Methodological Note, Luxembourg. Available from: https://ec.europa.eu/eurostat/web/experimental-statistics/qali.

Eurostat (2017-2022). *Sustainable Development in the European Union*, Overview of Progress Towards the SDGs in an EU Context, annual editions, Luxembourg. Available from: https://ec.europa.eu/eurostat/web/sdi.

Eurostat (2017a). *Environmental Protection Expenditure Accounts Handbook*, Luxembourg. Available from: https://seea.un.org/content/environmental-protection-expenditure-accounts-handbook-%E2%80%9--2017-edition.

Eurostat (2017b). *Integrated Framework for Environmental Activity Accounts*, 23rd London Group Meeting, Costa Rica. Available from: https://seea.un.org/sites/seea.un.org/files/lg23_document_integrated_framework_estat.pdf.

Eurostat (2018). *Integrated Framework for Environmental Activity Accounts*, Unit E-2: Environmental statistics and accounts; sustainable development, Note, Luxembourg. Available from: https://seea.un.org/sites/seea.un.org/files/seea_paper_integrated_framework_estat_v5.pdf.

Eurostat (2019a). *European Strategy for Environmental Accounts (ESEA) 2019-2023*, Luxembourg. Available from: https://ec.europa.eu/eurostat/web/environment/links.

Eurostat (2019b). *Manual on Sources and Methods for the Compilation of COFOG Statistics*, 3rd edition, Luxembourg. Available from: https://ec.europa.eu/eurostat/web/products-manuals-and-guidelines/-/ks-gq-19-010.

Eurostat (2019c). *Manual on Government Deficit and Debt — Implementation of ESA 2010*, Collection: Manuals and guidelines, Theme: Economy and finance, Luxembourg. Available from: https://ec.europa.eu/eurostat/en/web/products-manuals-and-guidelines/w/ks-gq-23-002.

Eurostat (2020). *Classification of Environmental Protection Activities and Expenditure (CEPA) and Classification of Resource Management Activities (CReMA) - Explanatory notes*, EEEA/2020/03, Technical Note, Luxembourg. Available from: https://ec.europa.eu/eurostat/web/environment/methodology.

Eurostat (2021). *European Strategy for Environmental Accounts (ESEA) - Mid-Term Review*, Luxembourg. Available from: https://ec.europa.eu/eurostat/documents/1798247/6191525/European+Strategy+for+Environmental+Accounts/.

Eurostat (2022). *Modernisation of EAA – Measurement of the economic value of public goods produced by the agricultural sector, 2022 edition*, Luxembourg. Available from: https://ec.europa.eu/eurostat/web/products-statistical-reports/w/ks-09-22-423.

Eurostat (2023). *Sustainable Development in the European Union, Monitoring Report on the Progress Towards the SDGS in an EU Context*, Luxembourg. Available from: https://ec.europa.eu/eurostat/documents.

FICCI (2014). *Corporate Sustainability: Drivers and Enablers*, India Sustainability Conclave, New Delhi. Available from: https://ficci.in/studies.asp.

Forum Terzo Settore (2017). *Il Terzo Settore e gli Obiettivi di Sviluppo Sostenibile*. Report, Rome. Available from: https://www.forumterzosettore.it/pubblicazioni/.

GASAB (2020). *Concept Paper on Natural Resource Accounting in India – An Initiative of GASAB*, New Delhi. Available from: http://gasab.gov.in/gasab/documents.aspx.

Gaspar, V., Medas, P. and Perrelli, R. (2021). *Global Debt Reaches a Record $226 Trillion*, IMF, Washington. Available from: https://www.imf.org/en.

Government of India (2011). *National Voluntary Guidelines on Social, Environmental and Economic Responsibilities of Business*, Ministry of Corporate Affairs, New Delhi. Available from: https://www.pib.gov.in/Pressreleaseshare.aspx?PRID=1568750&reg=3&lang=2.

Government of India (2019). *National Guidelines for Responsible Business Conduct*, Ministry of Corporate Affairs, New Delhi. Available from: https://www.mca.gov.in/Ministry/pdf/NationalGuildeline_15032019.pdf.

Government of India (2022). *Constitution of India*, Legislative Department, New Delhi. Available from: https://legislative.gov.in/constitution-of-india.

IARIW (2020). *Framework for a Satellite Account on the Digital Economy*, Updating the System of National Accounts to Reflect the Role of Digitalization, document, 14th Meeting of the ISWGNA, Ottawa. Available from: https://iariw.org/iariw-digital-session-on-the-sna-update-and-related-international-standards-wednesday-august-26-2020/.

ILO (2011). *Manual of the Measurement of Volunteer Work*, Geneva. Available from: https://www.ilo.org/publications/manual-measurement-volunteer-work.

InVEST (2022). *Natural Capital Project*, User Guide (online), Stanford. Available from: https://naturalcapitalproject.stanford.edu/software/invest.

IMF (2022). *World Economic Outlook Update*, Washington DC. Available from: https://www.imf.

org/en/Publications/WEO/Issues/2022/10/11/world-economic-outlook-october-2022.

IPCC (2019). *Global Warming of 1.5 °C*, Special Report, Geneva. Available from: https://www.ipcc.ch/sr15/.

IPCC (2023). *AR6 Synthesis Report: Climate Change 2022*, Report, Geneva. Available from: https://www.ipcc.ch/reports/.

ISO (2018). *Ecolabelling ISO 14024:2018, Environmental Labels and Declarations – Type I Environmental Labelling - Principles and Procedures*, 2nd edition, Geneva. Available from: https://www.iso.org/standard/72458.html.

ISTAT (1995). *Imprese, Istituzioni e Unità Locali. 1*, Fascicolo nazionale: Italia, Rome..

ISTAT (2014-2022). *Nonprofit Institutions Profile Based on Census Results*, Rome. Available from: https://www.istat.it/en/permanent-censuses/public-institutions.

ISTAT (2016). *Il Programma di Modernizzazione dell'Istat*, Rome. Available from: https://www.istat.it/it/files/2010/12/Programma_modernizzazione_Istat2016.pdf.

ISTAT (2020). *L'economia non Osservata nei Conti Nazionali – Anni 2015-2018*, Statistiche Report, Roma. Available from: https://www.istat.it/it/archivio/248596.

ISTAT (2021). *Il Conto dei Beni e Servizi Ambientali – Anni 2014-2017*, Statistiche Report, Roma. Available from: https://www.istat.it/it/archivio/227644.

KPMG (2020). *The Time Has Come: The KPMG Survey of Sustainability Reporting 2020*, Amstelveen. Available from: https://assets.kpmg/content/dam/kpmg/xx/pdf/2020/11/the-time-has-come.pdf.

Krugman, P. (1994). *The Age of Diminished Expectations*, MIT Press, Cambridge -Massachusetts. Available from: https://mitpress.mit.edu/9780262611343/the-age-of-diminished-expectations/.

Lorenz, E. (1972). *Predictability: Does the Flap of a Butterfly's Wings in Brazil Set Off a Tornado in Texas?* American Association for the Advancement of Sciences, 139th meeting, Washington. Published in Lorenz, E. (1993) The Essence of Chaos, University of Washington Press, Washington..

Mbaye, S., Moreno-Badia, M., and Chae. K. (2018). *Global Debt Database: Methodology and Sources*, IMF Working Paper, Washington. Available from: https://www.imf.org/en/Publications/WP/Issues/2018/05/14/Global-Debt-Database-Methodology-and-Sources-45838.
[http://dx.doi.org/10.5089/9781484353592.001]

Mokyr, J. (2008). *Technology*, in Palgrave Macmillan (eds) The New Palgrave Dictionary of Economics, Palgrave Macmillan, London. Available from: https://www.palgrave.com/us/campaigns/dictionary-of-economics.
[http://dx.doi.org/10.1057/978-1-349-95121-5_2739-1]

MoSPI (1998-2016). *Compendium of Environment Statistics*, various years, New Delhi. Available from: https://www.mospi.gov.in/web/mospi/reports-publications.

MoSPI (2006, 2008). *Natural Resource Accounting Report*, NRA Project, New Delhi. Available from: https://www.mospi.gov.in/web/mospi/reports-publications.

MoSPI (2013). *Green National Accounts in India* - A Framework, New Delhi. Available from: https://www.mospi.gov.in/web/mospi/reports-publications.

MoSPI (2020). *India Environmental Valuation Look-up (EVL) Tool*, User Guide, EFTEC, London. Available from: https://www.mospi.gov.in/web/mospi/india-evl-tool.

MoSPI (2021). *Ecosystem Accounts for India, Report of the NCAVES Project*, New Delhi. Available from: https://www.mospi.gov.in/web/mospi/reports-publications.

NSF (2019). *Statistics al a Crossroads*. Who is for the Challenges?, Ann Arbor. Available from: https://www.nsf.gov/mps/dms/documents/Statistics_at_a_Crossroads_Workshop_Report_2019.pdf.

NRC (2005). *Beyond the Market: Designing Nonmarket Accounts for the United States*, The National Academies Press, Washington. Available from: https://nap.nationalacademies.org/catalog/11181/beyond-the-market-designing-nonmarket-accounts-for-the-united-states.

OECD (2001). *Measuring Productivity. Measurement of Aggregate and Industrial-Level Productivity Growth*, Manual, Available from: https://www.oecd.org/sdd/productivity-stats/2352458.pdf.

OECD (2002). *Measuring the non-Observed Economy (NOE)*, Handbook, Paris. Available from: https://www.oecd-ilibrary.org/economics/measuring-the-non-observed-economy-a-handbook_9789264175358-en.

OECD (2011). *Towards Green Growth: A Summary for Policy Makers*, Paris. Available from: www.oecd.org/greengrowth.

OECD (2018). *Beyond GDP. Measuring What Counts for Economic and Social Performance*, Paris. Available from: https://www.oecd.org/wise/measurement-economic-social-progress.htm.

OECD (2021). *Classification of the Functions of Government (COFOG)*, in Government at a Glance 2021, Paris. Available from: https://www.oecd-ilibrary.org/governance/government-at-a-glance-2021_95603f6f-en.

OECD (2022). *Agricultural Total Factor Productivity and the Environment. A Guide to Emerging Best Practices in Measurement*, No. 177, Paris. Available from: https://www.oecd.org/agriculture/topics/network-agricultural-productivity-and-environment/.

OECD/WHO/EC (2017). *A System of Health Accounts (SHA) 2011*, revised edition, Manual, Paris. Available from: https://www.oecd.org/publications/a-system-of-health-accounts-2011-9789264270985-en.htm.

Pascarella, C. and Pisani, S. (2000). *Il Sommerso nelle Stime dell'Offerta*, ISTAT, Roma.

Pizzoli, E. (2020). *The Green Economy: a Technological Option Against Economic Crisis?*, in The 2008 Crisis Ten Years ON: in Retrospective, Context and Prospect, WEA Books, Bristol.

Putnam, R., Leonardi, R. and Nanetti, R. (1993). *Making Democracy Work: Civic Traditions in Modern Italy*, Princeton University Press, Princeton. Available from: https://press.princeton.edu/books/paperback/9780691037387/making-democracy-work.

Quintano, C. and Mazzocchi, P. (2008). *Una Visione d'Insieme sull'Economia Sommersa: Approcci, Contributi, Sperimentazioni*, Quaderno di discussione, n. 31, Scritti di statistica, Dipartimento di statistica e matematica per la ricerca economica, Università di Napoli 'Parthenope', Napoli.

Radermacher, W. J. (2020). *Official Statistics 4.0. Verified Facts for People in the 21st Century*, Springer, Berlin.
[http://dx.doi.org/10.1007/978-3-030-31492-7]

Rosenberg, N. (1983). *Inside the Black Box. Technology and Economics*, Cambridge University Press, Cambridge.

[http://dx.doi.org/10.1017/CBO9780511611940]

Salamon, L., Haddock, M. (2015). *SDGs and NPIs: Private non-Profit Institutions. The Foot Soldiers for the UN Sustainable Development Goals*, Johns Hopkins Center for Civil Society Studies Working Paper Series No. 25, 2015. Available from: http://ccss.jhu.edu/wp-content/uploads/downloads/2015/ 11/SDGs-NPIs_Salamon-Haddock_5.2015.pdf.

Salamon, L. (2016). *Putting NPIs and the Third Sector on the Economic Map of the World*, 47th Session of the United Nations Statistical Commission, New York. Available from: https://unstats.un.org/unsd/statcom/47th-session/documents/.

Schenau, S. (2016). *Research Agenda for the SEEA-CF*, 11th Meeting of UNCEEA, New York. Available from: https://unstats.un.org/unsd/envaccounting/ceea/meetings/eleventh_meeting/BK-11-3a.pdf.

Schneider, F. and Enste, D.H. (2000). *Shadow Economies: Size, Causes and Consequences*, Journal of Economic Literature, 38, 77-114, Pittsburgh.
[http://dx.doi.org/10.1257/jel.38.1.77]

Schumpeter, J. (1911). *Theorie der Wirtschaftlichen Entwicklung*, Verlag Duncker & Humblot, Leipzig, Germany.

SEBI (2020). *Consultation Paper on the Format for Business Responsibility and Sustainability Reporting*, New Delhi. Available from: https://www.sebi.gov.in/reports-and-statistics.html.

Stiglitz, J., Sen, A., Fitoussi, J-F. (2009). *Report by the Commission on the Measurement of Economic Performance and Social Progress*, Paris. Available from: https://ec.europa.eu/eurostat/documents/8131721/8131772/Stiglitz-Sen-Fitoussi-Commission-report.pdf.

UNSTAT (1980). *Classification of the Functions of Government*, Statistical Papers, Series No. 70, No. E.80.XVII.17, New York.

UNSTAT (1993). *System of National Accounts* 1993, New York. Available from: https://unstats.un.org/unsd/nationalaccount/sna1993.asp.

UNSTAT (2000). *Classifications of Expenditure According to Purpose: Classification of the Functions of Government (COFOG), Classification of Individual Consumption According to Purpose (COICOP), Classification of the Purposes of non-Profit Institutions Serving Households (COPNI), Classification of the Outlays of Producers According to Purpose (COPP)*, Statistical Papers, Series n. 85, New York.

UNSTAT (2014). *System of Environmental-Economic Accounting (SEEA) 2012. Central Framework*, New York. Available from: https://seea.un.org/content/seea-central-framework.

UNSTAT (2017). *The System of Environmental-Economic Accounting 2012 - Applications and Extensions*, New York. Available from: https://seea.un.org/applications-extensions.

UNSTAT (2024). *The System of Environmental-Economic Accounting - Ecosystem Accounting*, New York. Available from: https://seea.un.org/ecosystem-accounting.

UNSTAT (2024). *A World of Debt. A Growing Burden to Global Prosperity*, UN Global Crisis Response Group Report, New York. Available from: https://unctad.org/publication/world-of-debt.

UNEP (2017). *Green Industrial Policy: Concept, Policies, Country Experiences*, UN Environment Report, Nairobi. Available from: www.unenvironment.org/explore-topics/green-economy.

UNSTAT (2003). *Handbook on non-Profit Institutions in the System of National Accounts*, Series F., No. 91,

New York. Available from: https://digitallibrary.un.org/record/504170.

UNSTAT (2009). *System of National Accounts 2008*, New York. Available from: https://unstats.un.org/unsd/nationalaccount/sna.asp.

UNSTAT (2010). *Tourism Satellite Account: Recommended Methodological Framework 2008*, Studies in Methods, Series F No. 80/Rev.1, New York. Available from: https://unstats.un.org/UNSDWebsite/Publications.

UNSTAT (2017). *Framework for the Development of Environment Statistics (FDES 2013)*, Studies in Methods Series M No. 92, New York. Available from: https://unstats.un.org/unsd/envstats/fdes.cshtml.

UNSTAT (2018). *Satellite Account on non-Profit and Related Institutions and Volunteer Work*, Handbook of National Accounting, Studies in Methods, Series F, No. 91, Rev. 1, New York. Available from: https://unstats.un.org/unsd/nationalaccount/pubs.asp.

UNSTAT (2020). *A Broader Framework for Wellbeing and Sustainability in the System of National Accounts*, Guidance proposed by the Task Team on Wellbeing and Sustainability, 14th Meeting of the Advisory Expert Group on National Accounts, ISWGNA, New York Available from: https://unstats.un.org/unsd/nationalaccount/aeg.asp.

UNWTO (2019). *Sport Tourism and the Sustainable Development Goals (SDGs)*, Madrid. Available from: https://www.e-unwto.org/doi/epdf/.
[http://dx.doi.org/10.18111/9789284419661]

UNWTO (2000). *Recommendations on Tourism and Rural Development – A Guide to Making Tourism an Effective Tool for Rural Development*, Madrid. Available from: https://www.e-unwto.org/doi/epdf/.
[http://dx.doi.org/10.18111/9789284422173]

UNWTO (2021). *Inclusive Recovery Guide – Sociocultural Impacts of Covid-19*, Issue 3: Women in tourism, Madrid. Available from: https://www.e-unwto.org/.

WBSCD (2018). *Sustainability Reporting Landscape in India*, The Reporting Exchange, Geneva. Available from: https://www.wbcsd.org/contentwbc/download/5760/76829/1.

WEF (2022). *Global Risks Report 2022*, Zurich. .

WEBSITES

BEA

https://www.bea.gov/resources/learning-center/what-to-know-special-topics

Eurostat

https://ec.europa.eu/eurostat/web/government-finance-statistics

EU

https://eur-lex.europa.eu/

FENStatS

https://www.fenstats.eu/

IARNIW

https://iarniw.in/

ISTAT

1. https://www.istat.it/en/archive
2. https://www.istat.it/en/national-accounts
3. https://www.istat.it/en/well-being-and-sustainability
4. https://www.istat.it/en/environment-and-energy

SLS

https://luxstat.lu/

STATEC

https://statistiques.public.lu/

MoSPI

https://www.mospi.gov.in/web/mospi/reports-publications

OECD

https://www.oecd.org/wise/measurement-economic-social-progress.htm

UNEP

https://www.unenvironment.org

UNSTAT

1. https://unstats.un.org/unsd/nationalaccount/

2. https://unstats.un.org/unsd/nationalaccount/towards2025.asp

3. https://seea.un.org/

SUBJECT INDEX

A

B

C

D

E

O

P

Q

R

S

T

U

W

Z

www.ingramcontent.com/pod-product-compliance
Ingram Content Group UK Ltd.
Pitfield, Milton Keynes, MK11 3LW, UK
UKHW062211071026
15591UKWH00020B/140
9798898813598